Compliments of

#antisemitism

#antisemitism

Coming of Age during the Resurgence of Hate

Samantha A. Vinokor-Meinrath

PRAEGER®

An Imprint of ABC-CLIO, LLC

Santa Barbara, California • Denver, Colorado

Library of Congress Control Number: 2022904954

ISBN: 978-1-4408-7899-2 (print)
       978-1-4408-7900-5 (ebook)

26 25 24 23 22   1 2 3 4 5

This book is also available as an eBook.

Praeger
An Imprint of ABC-CLIO, LLC

ABC-CLIO, LLC
147 Castilian Drive
Santa Barbara, California 93117
www.abc-clio.com

This book is printed on acid-free paper ∞
Manufactured in the United States of America

This book is dedicated to the memories of Regina (Rechla) Adler Fried-mann Wachtel, Ruth Friedmann, and Hella Sabine Friedmann. Growing up, I knew that my beloved Grandma Rita was a child of the Holocaust, an awareness that ultimately set me on the journey that became this book. Rita Adler Kreinin was born to a large Polish Jewish family in Berlin, a family with five children. Ultimately, three survived and emigrated to the United States: my great-grandfather, Markus Adler, and two of his broth-ers. Another brother, Leo, was murdered for being a Jew, a story that is recounted later in this book. But the memory that was almost forgotten was that of Regina, the only sister, who stayed in Berlin, and, together with her daughters, was deported to Riga, Latvia, where all three were ultimately shot in a mass grave in the Rumbula and Bikernieki Forests in October 1942.

Historian Ian Kershaw said, "The road to Auschwitz was built by hate but paved with indifference." My hope for Generation Z, which is shared by those of us who care deeply about its members, is that instead of indif-ference, they will commit themselves to making a difference and standing up to hate. By remembering Regina and her teenage daughters—my cous-ins who never had a chance to grow into women who could have changed the world—and by working to build a better reality for future generations, I hope that this book will touch others and inspire partners and allies in this sacred work.

May the memories of Regina, Ruth, and Hella be for a blessing.

Contents

Introduction   ix

ONE   Jewish Generation Z: Who/What/Where/Why   1

TWO   Never Again: The Burden of the Last Generation
         to Meet Holocaust Survivors   18

THREE   #Jewish: Telling Their Stories via Social Media   39

FOUR   Pittsburgh: The Day Safety Ended   55

FIVE   The Dyke March: How Anti-Israelism
         Becomes Antisemitism   68

SIX   Jewish Stars, Shirts, and Swag   90

SEVEN   But You Don't *Look* Jewish: Diversity
         within the Jewish Community   102

EIGHT   What about Mom and Dad?   112

NINE   Proud but Uncertain: Jewish Identity
         and Self Definitions   122

TEN   Where Do We Go from Here?   145

Appendix A Learning Guide for Jewish Communities   155

Appendix B Learning Guide for Allies   159

Index   163

Introduction

Growing up, like most kids I found my friends based on a few key factors: Were they nice? Did they like reading, arts and crafts, or jump rope? Were we in the same class? And most important, if I, as a Jewish girl, needed to go into hiding, would they provide that safe haven?

As a child, I went through a phase when I was obsessed with fire safety. Spurred by an elementary school curriculum that included a trip to the local firehouse, I channeled my passion into developing a family escape plan. I prepared a meeting spot across the street, a roll-away ladder under my bed (the better for breaking out of my second-story window), and a pink, patterned go-bag. Inside the monogrammed bag, I placed my most prized possessions: the diary chronicling my suburban trials and tribulations, a family photo, my favorite book, and a stuffed animal. I placed the bag right next to my bed for safekeeping, ready to be taken with me should a quick escape be necessary. This quirk, like my brother's desire to become a pirate or my sister's phase of carrying a straw basket full of snow globes everywhere she went, was accepted and indulged, eventually becoming a charming anecdote of a lovely childhood.

The next stage of this phase was a little different.

I stopped being concerned about fire as an imminent danger to my home and gave up on the spontaneous evacuation drills, but I still couldn't give up my go-bag. It never stopped seeming critically important to have my most cherished items collected and ready to go at a moment's notice.

Why was this necessary for a girl from a loving family, living a comfortable and privileged life in suburban Long Island in the 1990s?

Obviously, it was because of the Nazis.

As a precocious and avid reader, I had been introduced to these shadowy figures early on. I knew the basics: they were bad people who could show up at any time, forcing the Jewish character (usually a young heroine to whom I related immediately) to leave her home and go into hiding or be sent to a camp. Nazis were the mysterious men who might take away your grandparents and leave you alone, without a family or a home. Without any broader historical context, it seemed only logical that I, as a Jewish girl, should be ready to run from the Nazis. Because who wanted to be taken by surprise if it ever happened?

As one might imagine, this phase was slightly less indulged than the fire safety era, and my parents were quick to reassure me that the time when the Jewish people needed to be afraid was long over. I had nothing to worry about. For years, this proved to be the case. Thanks to Jewish youth movements and numerous trips to Israel, I regularly wore Jewish stars, Israel Defense Forces T-shirts, and United Synagogue Youth sweatshirts to school, sometimes all at once. I was a vocal and proud Jew, always eager to learn more and confident in my knowledge and identity. My early Holocaust fears gave way to a sense of security in my role as an emerging Jewish leader, a label that was applied to me by my rabbi, my youth group director, and numerous other role models. I relished the fact that when having Shabbat dinner with my family or traveling to Israel with my friends, I was somehow connected to something larger than myself. When I was practicing my Judaism, I was carrying out the battle cry of Never Again. Jewish kids like me would never live in fear of expulsion. They would never have to subconsciously evaluate their non-Jewish friends, wondering on some primal level, "Could I hide in their house if the Nazis came for me?" They would never have to worry about tucking Jewish star necklaces into their shirt collars on subways or removing yarmulkes from their heads. That time was over, and now we could breathe easily.

As my teachers and mentors predicted, I eventually became a Jewish educator. As soon as I learned that I could translate my passion for Jewish learning into a career, my future was set. I even chose to specialize in working with high school students because of how formative that period had been for me personally. In my public high school, I did my best to fit in but always found myself on the fringes. My Jewish teen experience was the complete opposite. I learned how to be the best version of myself in the Jewish community, and it was a dream come true to realize that I could help the next generation achieve that as well.

In my work with Jewish teens, I found Generation Z to be significantly different from my millennial peers. Generation Z, born in the late 1990s and early 2000s, is the first generation to be born "digital natives." They were born into a time of unprecedented growth in technology and connectivity. At the same time, their lives have been marked by school shootings, climate uncertainty and change, divisive politics, and ever-evolving questions of identity and allegiance. They have grown up in the shadow of 9/11 and its aftermath, having never experienced a time when the United States was not at war. And for Jewish Generation Zers in particular, their formative years are now being shaped by a resurgence of antisemitism. They are a generation with access and the power to act. As Claire Sarnowski, whom we will get to know later, shared, "Everyone can be an activist. You don't have to be on the news or even to get recognized in order to make a difference." This confidence in the power of mission, access, and capacity demonstrates a generation that is ready to take on the world.

While they may only be separated by a few years, the demographically adjacent generations of millennials and Generation Z answer questions about Jewish identity in markedly different ways. When millennials are asked if they feel comfortable in a Jewish space, they tend to answer in terms of emotional comfort: Were they welcomed? Was the language inclusive, the opinions diverse, the narratives affirming of their identities? But when I asked Generation Zers if they felt comfortable in Jewish spaces, they spoke about increased security presence, active shooter drills, and self-defense. For Generation Z, comfort means physical security, because they live in a world—both Jewishly and otherwise—where their safety cannot be taken for granted.

This reality has only been augmented by the resurgence in antisemitism that has come as a result of various elements, including the emboldenment of white nationalism in the United States, the divisive rhetoric of the Trump administration, cancel culture on the political Left, and the COVID-19 coronavirus pandemic. Each of these respective national and global realities has morphed antisemitism to meet its ends while retaining links to a hatred that has spanned generations. With the advent of the COVID-19 pandemic, there came a new form of an ancient libel: blaming Jews for the global spread of the virus.[1] This latest scapegoating of the Jewish people is at once new, responding to the latest global reality, and age-old. Placing the onus on Jews for a plague and the spread of a disease goes back to the Black Death, which decimated Europe from 1348 to 1351.[2] For Jewish Generation Zers, for whom the pandemic has derailed school, the start of careers, and seminal social experiences and rites of passage, the added anxiety of being blamed for such tragedies can be assumed to have lasting effects on their still-developing Jewish psyches.

Many Generation Zers know all too well the uncomfortable silence that serves as the aftermath of realizing that you've been hit with an antisemitic incident and needing to process how to respond and what to do next. Jenny, from Boston, shared that sometimes she experiences denial. "Sometimes I don't want to accept that what someone is saying is antisemitic, so I just don't let it register in my mind." She has a memory of a classmate walking up to her in the hall during her freshman year of high school, and saying, "Hey, Jen, you're Jewish, right?" When she answered in the affirmative, the response was, "Don't worry. I still like you." Ella, from Los Angeles, remembers a boy telling her, "You're hot for a Jewish girl." For many Generation Zers, these awkward encounters can leave them reeling, particularly when they relate to Israel. As Ella shared, "People aren't prepared or confident in dealing with antisemitism. There was an incident in my school where a teacher was using a Hitler meme, and all the other Jewish kids reached out to me to ask me how to deal with it. When it's just you by yourself, it's easy to just want to ignore it and shut down instead of engaging."

Antisemitism is confusing in its complexity. In one of the most apt analogies I've heard used, this ever-evolving and constantly morphing hatred of the Jewish people was compared to the boggart in J. K. Rowling's Harry Potter book series. The boggart, a magical creature, is a shape-shifter that will assume the form of whatever the person who encounters it is the most frightened of.[3] So, too, is the nature of antisemitism. It defies logic, reason, and rationality. Instead, in every place, and seemingly in every generation, antisemitism emerges in a way that feeds into the fears of the populace. In medieval Europe, antisemitism stemmed from religion, with the Jews being accused of deicide, having collective responsibility for the death of Jesus as described in the Gospels.[4] In Germany in the years leading up to World War II, Jews became the scapegoat for the financial distress that the country was in during the interwar years.[5] And in the United States of 2020, an increasingly polarized society found multiple ways to explain the vocalization of once latent antisemitism. Dual loyalty,[6] Jews as financial puppet masters secretly controlling the economy and the government,[7] Israel as an abuser of human rights,[8] and countless other accusations have been vocalized by members of the political Left, the Right, and the armchair activists of the internet. During the COVID-19 pandemic, antisemitism in the United States saw a new twist, with accusations coming from both the far Left and the Right.[9] Amanda Berman, whom we will learn more about later, noted that "antisemitism from the Left and the Right are actually very similar. Antisemitism in general manifests as conspiracy theories. But if we spend our time saying that antisemitism is worse 'over there,' then we don't actually have to deal with it in our own spaces."

The changing and volatile nature of antisemitism and its varying manifestations, both over time and simultaneously at this juncture in history, can be confusing and frightening, particularly for adolescents and emerging adults. To be at a life stage of trying to figure out where you stand in relation to your faith and cultural identity in the first place,[10] and then to have a sense of attack, can fundamentally shape the lifelong relationship that this generation will have with Judaism. Whether they will lean further into it, pull away, or find new ways to relate to their Jewish identities, the growing shape-shifting specter of antisemitism is an undeniable factor in the Jewish experience of American Jewish life. It can manifest as microaggressions that may not even be recognized as antisemitism at the moment. Bailey, a college student, counts among her first Jewish memories being given the elementary school art project of making Christmas stockings and knowing that it wasn't something that her family or her faith had a practice of. But she was told by the teacher that it wasn't "religious" and had her discomfort invalidated. "From an early age, it felt like I was being told that it was impossible to belong because the community I was in was set up in a way that inherently excluded me because of my identity." Rebecca, a Texan whom we will hear from again later, also has childhood memories of antisemitism, though her experiences were of a more direct nature than Bailey's. "I grew up hearing kids tell me that I was going to go to hell [because I don't believe in Jesus]. I always have to have the last word, so I'd be sarcastic and say, 'Yeah, I have to reclaim my throne.' I never let them see that it hits me. It absolutely does, and it hurts, and tears are shed, but I never let them see it. If they see my reaction to it, then they win."

It has been said that hatred of Jews is the most acceptable form of hatred toward other people. And the unfortunate reality is that hatred as a whole is on the rise in the United States. According to data collected from 6,506 institutions of higher education by the U.S. Department of Education, the number of reported hate incidents on campuses increased from 74 in 2006 to 1,300 in 2016.[11] Vandalism and intimidation account for 76 percent of these reported incidents. The most well-known and infamous incident of hatred on a college campus is elements of the 2017 Unite the Right rally in Charlottesville, Virginia, which ultimately left one individual dead.

On August 11, 2017, a group of white nationalists marched through the University of Virginia's campus, chanting Nazi and white supremacist slogans:

White Lives Matter
Jews will not replace us
Blood and Soil [12]

The group of white nationalist marchers, most of whom had traveled to Charlottesville for the following day's planned Unite the Right rally, encountered University of Virginia students staging a counterprotest. A fight broke out, ultimately preceding the official rally the following day, which led to a state of emergency being declared by Virginia's governor, and the tragic death of Heather D. Heyer, who was protesting the hateful rhetoric of the rally.

The Unite the Right rally was a watershed moment of hatred in the United States, but it by no means stands alone. During the first quarter of 2021, the Center for the Study of Hate & Extremism at California State University, San Bernardino, found that hate crimes against Asian Americans had increased by a staggering 169 percent.[13] 2019 saw 51 hate crime–based murders, according to the FBI.[14] As of 2020, there were 566 extreme antigovernment groups operating in the United States, with 169 having the designation of active militias.[15] It is clear that antisemitism does not stand alone as a rising and legitimate threat within the United States. However, antisemitism remains, in many ways, unique.

In 2009, Ambassador Janez Lenarčič, then the director of the OSCE Office for Democratic Institutions and Human Rights, said, "The level of antisemitism in a country is an important barometer of the general level of tolerance and openness towards diversity in society. When antisemitism is on the rise, other ethnic or religious groups may also face acts of hatred and intolerance."[16] The increase of antisemitism in the United States comes in tandem with the rise in hatred and acts of violence and intimidation against minority groups as a whole. Despite the increasing diversity of the American population, and in many ways the increase of acceptance of differences between peoples, the undercurrent of hatred that manifests in antisemitism has spilled over in both extreme and subtle ways that have colored the American experience.

Discerning what "counts" as antisemitism can often be a complex, deeply personal process. Nora, a college student from Connecticut, shared that she is sometimes hesitant about naming particular experiences and incidents as outright antisemitism. "In the Jewish community, we're sometimes trigger-happy in calling something antisemitism. We feel like we need to defend ourselves, and we're eager to define things that happen as antisemitism. I have a problem with that, so I'm sometimes hesitant to call something antisemitism. I'm just not always that confident in defining it." While sometimes there are black-and-white examples of antisemitism, something that too many Generation Zers, including Nora herself, have experienced, often there is a gray area where decisions about what crosses the line need to be made.

For the last ten years, I've had the honor and sacred responsibility of educating Jewish teens. I've had the chance to get to know this next generation—their dreams, their fears, the pressures they feel internally and externally. The role of the Jewish educator is marked by its multi-faceted nature. I have worn the hats of counselor (camp, college, and life), event planner, teacher, spiritual advisor, big sister, mom, rule enforcer, marketer, and tour guide. I've held the hands of girls overwhelmed with first love and first heartbreak. I've listened to boys grapple with what it means to be a man and how to reconcile their inner and outer selves in ways that feel authentic yet will be accepted by their peers. And I've been a thought partner as these young people explore how their Jewish identities manifest and what role this aspect of their intersectional identities will play in shaping their lives.

There have been high points, moments of pride. I've sat under a night sky at a campground, asking shared questions about morality and personal responsibility, hearing from the next generation of mystics as they pieced together emerging worldviews and tried to make sense of the world around them. I've shared seats on long bus rides that have been places of plotting future goals and have been present at the birth of ideas that, should they come to fruition, will surely change the world. I've seen leaders blossom, nurturers evolve, and countless adolescents come into their own as well-rounded, complex individuals, ready to take on the challenges that life has, and will surely continue to, throw at them.

But I've also held back my own tears as teens have come to me with questions in their eyes about hate, prejudice, and senseless anger. What does one say when they're asked to make sense of a teacher who shut down the voice of a Jewish student, telling the student that there's no conclusive evidence of the murder of over six million Jews during the Holocaust? Or when they're charged with helping a teen respond to someone who used a "pickup line" as abhorrent as, "How do you get a Jewish girl's number? Check the inside of her arm." How do you fill the silence that comes when the black mark of a swastika leaves the pages of history books and finds its way onto a locker or a notebook or the home of adolescents just trying to find their place in the world?

I've made choices in each of these instances. They may not always have been the right ones or the ones that each of the educators I'll profile in this book would make. And ultimately, I think that's OK. To educate the Jewish teens of Generation Z is to operate in largely uncharted territory. It's to join them in a new world—one where social media is the barometer for legitimacy and social distancing is understood by nomenclature. It's a place where identities are complex and overlapping and everyone is responsible for making the world a better place—whatever that means. Generation Zers as a whole are living in the most diverse iteration of the United States that there has ever been. They're also living in one of the most polarized times in the collective memory of the American people. Jewish Generation Zers in particular are entering emerging adulthood against this backdrop, with the added baggage of coming to terms with a resurgence in antisemitism that has left the American Jewish community searching for new answers to ancient questions.

Rabbi David Wolpe wrote a blog post posing the query, Why do some people hate Jews? In his answer to this perennial question, he gave voice to the irrational, constantly evolving reality of antisemitism:

> Jews have been hated when they were poor and when they were rich; when they were communists and when they were capitalists; when they were stateless and when they had a state; when they were religious and when they were secular; when they 'invaded and took jobs' and when they were rootless and barred from the marketplace; when they were phenomenal achievers in the world and when they stayed in the study hall and did nothing but learn; even when they were present and (often after their expulsions and murders) when they no longer lived in the country that still bore hatred for them.
>
> In other words, Jews have been hated because they remained Jews. Because they refused, in the face of the most furious persecutions, to cease being who they were. Because they reflect back on the world the reality of its own brutality.[17]

Antisemitism is not rational. It isn't founded in a particular ideology, worldview, or school of thought. It's an ever-changing, constantly morphing reality that reconstitutes itself to prey on the weak points and gaps in any society. In the United States of the 2000s, it has diversified, manifesting on the political Left and Right, and adapting to various subsets of a multifaceted society.

Zeke, a high school sophomore from the Washington, DC, suburbs, reflected on the antisemitism that he and his peers are encountering in their schools, on social media, and in the United States as a whole. "We have antisemitism on the Left, like the BDS[18] movement. And while Generation Z is fighting with the Left on antisemitism, the Right is looming in the corner. They're the reason we have guards outside of our synagogues and why there's bulletproof glass funded by the government on the windows of my school." In this book, we will explore what it means to come of age as a Jewish young adult in an era marked by increasing antisemitism. We will meet the individuals who exist at the intersection of increased Jewish pride, elevated levels of fear, and unprecedented access to different voices through social media. Through the eyes of these Jewish Generation Zers, we will see how identities are shaped in response to and in defiance of antisemitism and what the diverse voices of American Jews are saying in response to this new reality. We will also place antisemitism into the context of the other trends impacting American society and how the Jewish experience factors into the national lexicon. Nora, the college student from Connecticut, noted that in her experience, the way that antisemitism is responded to can feel similar to how society reacts to sexual harassment. "It's allowed to continue in a really bizarre way, even though we know it's wrong. People and organizations aren't interested in taking the steps they would need to in order to really change things."

As a Jewish community, and as a larger American community, a great deal of emphasis is placed on education regarding how to respond to antisemitic acts and sentiments. Jewish teens and emerging adults are regularly offered the chance to participate in seminars and leadership training programs centered around standing up, speaking out, and determining tactics for responding to targeted hate. But there is a distinct lack of proactive work toward systemic change. Collectively, we have not done a great deal to educate the perpetrators of antisemitism on how to change.

As an educator, I have spent a great deal of time thinking about what success means for me as I share knowledge, experiences, and meaning-making opportunities with my learners. There are plenty of easy answers—I'm successful if they find meaning in my words and the lessons I guide them through, and if the experience is fun, and if when they think back on their Jewish educational encounters later in life, it's with positive feelings. I believe all of those things. But what drives me at my core is the goal for them to crave what's next. I never want my learners to be satisfied, to walk away from our time together with the mindset that they've somehow checked Jewish education off of their to-do lists and can now count themselves knowledgeable and move on. Instead, my goal is to leave every learner I encounter seeking more. I see my role as an educator as being that of sparking interest, connection, and next steps. I do not seek to provide exhaustive knowledge on any topic, and this book is no different. It is a snapshot in time, at a critical and unprecedented moment in American history. I have sought to provide multiple perspectives, insights from the breadth and depth of Jewish Generation Zers and those who care about them. There will inevitably be voices that are underserved, and while these omissions are not purposeful, my hope is that they pave the way for other voices to fill the gaps, contributing their own stories to the unfolding conversation about antisemitism.

NOTES

1. Winer, S. (2020, June 23). COVID-19 fueling worldwide wave of anti-Semitism, researchers find. *The Times of Israel.* Retrieved from https://www.timesofisrael.com/covid-19-fueling-worldwide-wave-of-anti-semitism-researchers-find

2. Brackman, H. (2020). Deadly new virus intersects with history's oldest hate: Report and analysis. The Simon Wiesenthal Center. Retrieved from https://www.wiesenthal.com/assets/pdf/deadly-new-virus-intersects.pdf

3. Rowling, J. K. (2015, August 10). Boggart. Wizarding World. Retrieved from https://www.wizardingworld.com/writing-by-jk-rowling/boggart

4. Fried, J. (2015). *The Middle Ages.* Cambridge, MA: Harvard University Press, pp. 287–289.

5. Brustein, W. I., & King, R. D. (2004). Anti-semitism in Europe before the Holocaust. *International Political Science Review, 25*(1), 35–53.

6. Emanuel, R. (2019, March 7). I've faced the charge of dual loyalty. *The Atlantic.*

7. Burton, T. I. (2018, November 2). The centuries-old history of Jewish "puppet master" conspiracy theories. Vox. Retrieved from https://www.vox.com/2018/11/2/15946556/antisemitism-enlightenment-george-soros-conspiracy-theory-globalist

8. American Jewish Committee (2021, April 28). 5 things you should know about Human Rights Watch's report on Israel. American Jewish Committee. Retrieved from https://www.ajc.org/news/5-things-you-should-know-about-human-rights-watchs-report-on-israel

9. Ministry of Diaspora Affairs (2021, January 27). Antisemitism annual report 2020. Ministry of Diaspora Affairs. Retrieved from https://www.gov.il/BlobFolder/generalpage/report_anti240121/en/anti-semitism_2020%20YEARLY%20REPORT%20-%20FINAL%20(EN)_v7.pdf

10. Fowler, J. W., & Dell, M. L. (2004). Stages of faith and identity: Birth to teens. *Child and Adolescent Psychiatric Clinics of North America, 13*(1), 17–33. Retrieved from https://doi.org/10.1016/S1056-4993(03)00073-7

11. U.S. Department of Education, Office of Postsecondary Education (n.d.). How many hate crimes were reported? Retrieved from https://ope.ed.gov/campussafety/Trend/public/#/answer/2/201/main

12. Chia, J. (2017, August 12). White nationalists march through UVA with torches. *Daily News.*

13. Yam, K. (2021, April 28). New report finds 169 percent surge in anti-Asian hate crimes during the first quarter. NBC News. Retrieved from https://www.nbcnews.com/news/asian-america/new-report-finds-169-percent-surge-anti-asian-hate-crimes-n1265756

14. Balsamo, M. (2020, November 16). Hate crimes in US reach highest level in more than a decade. AP News. Retrieved from https://apnews.com/article/hate-crimes-rise-FBI-data-ebbcadca8458aba96575da905650120d

15. Southern Poverty Law Center (n.d.). Antigovernment movement. Retrieved from https://www.splcenter.org/fighting-hate/extremist-files/ideology/antigovernment

16. Lenarčič, J. (2009, March 5). Launch of teaching tools to combat anti-Semitism for Polish secondary schools. OSCE Office for Democratic Institutions and Human Rights. Retrieved from https://www.osce.org/files/f/documents/2/7/36369.pdf

17. Wolpe, D. (2021, April 22). Why do some people hate Jews? *Times of Israel.* Retrieved from https://blogs.timesofisrael.com/why-do-some-people-hate-jews/H

18. Boycott, Divestment, and Sanctions.

ONE

Jewish Generation Z: Who/What/ Where/Why

When other Jews are trying to suss out how religious I am, they want to know whether I keep kosher, observe Shabbat, and am a member of a synagogue. These are questions about what I do, not what I believe.

—Sarah Hurwitz, *Here All Along: Finding Meaning, Spirituality, and a Deeper Connection to Life—In Judaism (After Finally Choosing to Look There)*

"Being Jewish for me isn't about what you believe, or God, or any of that. A lot of being Jewish is doubting God. It's the community and the people you're with and the things you do that make you Jewish."

Elana is a high school freshman in the Washington, DC, suburbs. In many ways, she's typical. She's an overachiever. She is close to her family and calls her mom her best friend. If you let her get started talking about her summer camp, she'll wax poetic for hours on end. And like thousands of her peers, she spends her time perfecting TikTok dances and stressing over the college admissions process, and she is more concerned about making the varsity field hockey team than she is about existential questions of her identity. But beneath the bubbly, quick-to-giggle surface, she's in the throes of an identity transformation as she explores what it means for her to have come of age as a young Jewish woman in the United States of 2020. In her childhood, Judaism was something fun. It meant presents on Chanukah, Shabbat dinners surrounded by family and food, and a network of friends, thanks to her summer camp. It brought challenges, of course. There were the numerous reminders she had to give to her teachers every year about why she couldn't do homework or wouldn't be in class on Jewish holidays. The well-meaning sympathy that classmates gave her when she told them she didn't have a Christmas tree. But nothing that she couldn't handle.

Elana proudly walked through her school, the shopping mall in her town, and airports wearing a Jewish star necklace and a T-shirt that proclaimed "Everybody Loves a Jewish Girl." She was excited to invite non-Jewish classmates to her bat mitzvah, smiled at Jewish references on her favorite TV shows, and laughed at the occasional Jewish joke. But in October 2018, her proud equilibrium fundamentally shifted when she scrolled through her Instagram feed and saw the initial reports of the shooting at Congregation Tree of Life in Pittsburgh, Pennsylvania. Elana didn't know anyone directly impacted by the massacre, the deadliest attack on the Jewish community in the history of the United States. She had never been to Pittsburgh. But she couldn't stop refreshing her feed, unable to look away from the rising death toll, the pain, and the shock. "I never felt targeted as a Jew before. I knew that I was connected to Jews around the world and that we had things in common, but the Pittsburgh shooting made things different. Everyone started talking about security guards and protecting ourselves. I guess I never felt like I needed protection before."

To be an American Jewish teen in the 2020s is to live in a world of dichotomies. There are more choices than ever before. More ways to "do Jewish" and for Jewish teens to get involved on their own terms than any previous generation has enjoyed. More leadership opportunities, travel experiences, and tailor-made options, all with the shared goal of connecting teens with Judaism, the Jewish community, and their own identities. And yet, in the face of abundant opportunities, teens still opt out of Jewish life in droves. In 2017, the Washington, DC, area reported that more than half of eligible Jewish children, that is, children with at least one Jewish-identifying parent, participated in some form of Jewish education through eighth grade. However, immediately afterward, during a transition time marked by the celebration of the *b'nai mitzvah* rite of passage and the entry to high school, that number drops to 17 percent. This number mirrors national trends and tells us that during the pivotal identity-building years of adolescence, over 80 percent of Jewish teens are not engaged in Jewish education.

There are those who despair as they look at the numbers of unengaged Jewish teens. Educators, clergy, parents, grandparents, and communal leaders of every stream spend time, capital, and excessive amounts of energy trying to solve the so-called question of how to keep the next generation engaged. It's inherent in Judaism to be preoccupied with the development of future generations. Indeed, this concern with passing on the values of Judaism and enculturating children to carry them on is canonized into Jewish texts, rituals, and commandments. The Passover seder, the most observed Jewish holiday rite in any given year, is centered around the perennial charge: you shall teach your children. Each generation of the Jewish people is called to answer that charge in a way that is reflective of its moment in history. For the educators, parents, and others concerned about Generation Z, there is therefore the question: What are we teaching, and what will success look like?

Rabbi Abbi, the mother of a Generation Zer and a member of Generation Alpha,[1] described success in terms of instilling a strong Jewish identity in her children this way: "I want my kids to feel proud of being Jewish and to be able to engage in a Judaism that is relevant and meaningful. I want them to be able to walk down the street and to say, 'I'm Jewish,' and to know what that means." She wants her children to connect with their Judaism in positive ways and to have some level of Jewish observance—"whatever that means"—as well as to raise Jewish families—"however that happens."

Nicki, a mother of three whom we will get to know in more detail later, sees success as "Judaism being an obligation but not a burden in my kids' lives. I see college students today who will say they're only Jewish inside their homes and in these little bubbles. But they don't want to put up signs advertising Hillel events or show their Judaism outside of those limited spaces. I want my kids to be comfortable being Jewish wherever they are."

Mara, a college student at SUNY Binghamton, reflected on the impact that her years of multifaceted Jewish education, including day school, camp, synagogue life, and youth group participation, as well as lively conversations around her own dining room table, had on her worldview. "My optimism has been informed by my Jewish values, the things that I was taught, and the idea that we're on an upward trajectory toward making the world a more whole place. There's this idea of there being a spark in every person in the world, and I get chills just thinking about it." A drive to change the world with a Jewish lens as the inspiration is compelling as a measurement of success in Jewish education. For Mara and many of her peers, to "do Jewish" is not limited to actions or environments that would necessarily be defined as traditionally Jewish, nor by elements that are limited to the Jewish people. Rather, Generation Zers are often deeply committed to universalist values to the point of prioritizing them over Jewish particularism. For some, this may be a cause for concern. Miriam, a Jewish communal professional and mother of a Generation Zer, spoke about the conflict of universalism and particularism as it pertains to philanthropic giving and personal donations of *tzedakah*, or charity. "If there's a Jewish option and you're not taking it, like if you're giving to the International Rescue Committee as opposed to the Hebrew Immigrant Aid Society, there's something broken." On the other hand, Lisa, whose professional background focuses on the teaching of the Holocaust in public schools, expressed an affinity for the universalist instincts of Generation Z. "I want my students to realize, just like I have obligations to my family and my immediate circles, I have obligations to the community beyond my family too. We each need to ask, who is in my universe of obligation?"

Generation Zers, growing up in an increasingly diverse, open, and yet polarized society, are answering these questions and dilemmas in unprecedented ways. This demographic cohort is collectively inheriting a world unlike that which has existed at any other historical juncture. Amanda Berman, the founder and executive director of Zioness, whom we will hear from throughout this book, noted that "there are threats to all marginalized communities." As a result, while in many ways the experiences of the Jewish community are unique due to a variety of factors that we will continue to explore, in other aspects, Jewish Generation Zers have joined their peers in a collective reckoning process, which started long ago but has been triggered into overdrive during the COVID-19 pandemic.

In 2008, before Generation Z had received its demographic moniker, Jewish educational thought leaders asked the question, Are we ready for the "post-millennials"? They described this generation, who at that point ranged from nursery to elementary schoolers, thus:

> These are the children of 9/11. They are growing up in a world marked by apparently irrational conflicts and sudden violence. Economic and environmental prospects are also uncertain and anxiety-producing. The United States and the West no longer rule an orderly domain making steady progress toward "freedom and democracy." The world as a whole has become more visibly diverse and intermingled. Boundaries are blurring, and as a reaction some are seeking and embracing new/old certainties and absolutes. Others, repelled by the violent by-products of this quest, try to negotiate between and

among competing truths and visions, and find themselves struggling to find solid moral ground.[2]

Looking back from the lens of 2021, the voices of 2008 seem to have been almost prophetic. The teens of Generation Z live in a world that is no longer contingent on the status quo of previous generations. They live in the most diverse United States that there has ever been.[3] They are on the cutting edge of new technology and of social movements built to create change and dismantle preexisting boundaries and norms. Colloquially referred to as the iGeneration,[4] they have come of age with the breadth and depth of human knowledge literally in the palms of their hands. They are savvy and adept at expressing themselves using the platforms that social media has made available to them. But the sophistication that comes from curating an identity that encourages engagement and likes, and creating hashtags and campaigns meant to inspire activism and solidarity, does not necessarily correlate with meaningfully dealing with the complexities of coming of age when your identity is being attacked on multiple fronts.

Jess, an older Generation Zer whom we will meet later, spoke about her experiences of antisemitism as a public high school student in the Northeast. "In high school, there were always Jew jokes—the nose or the counting pennies—but I don't think it impacted me as much, mostly because I was able to laugh at it. When everyone is saying something, you're pretty much left laughing along and saying 'Yeah, we do have big noses, or we do like money—who doesn't?' If something like that happened now, I would flip out. But I wasn't in a position to take a stand like that when I was sixteen." Like many other Generation Zers, and adolescents of any generation, Jess's concerns centered around fitting in and being a good sport. It was only later on that she came to terms with the internalized antisemitism that incidents of casual, humorous jokes at her expense had wrought and sought to do differently.

Matt, a high school senior from Maryland, is proud of his Judaism but doesn't actively engage in Jewish life. He goes to synagogue with his parents on Rosh Hashanah and Yom Kippur and remembers the blessings that he learned during the hours of study for his bar mitzvah. But his focus is mostly on getting accepted to his dream college, a source of contention with his parents. His dad is a fan of state universities, at least for the first two years, so he can save money before figuring out a major and a career path. His mom loves the idea of him staying closer to home but understands that he wants to spread his wings. Her biggest fear is centered around his dream school being in the South.

"We've already had incidents. He gets called Jew Boy on SnapChat. And he's a confident kid, so he laughs it off. And we had a social studies teacher who skipped the whole chapter on the Holocaust because it wasn't going to be on the test. Matt was too embarrassed for me to say anything to the principal, but it made me so angry that this wasn't being taught in schools. I think we've done a good job of teaching him to be proud. But then I heard him and his friends playing a video game and they called him a cheap Jew. And he laughed again. What if something worse happens?"

With social media as a breeding ground for antisemitic incidents, and Holocaust education only mandated in fifteen states, misinformation and a lack of information color the lived experiences of Jewish Generation Zers. For his part, Matt acknowledges that some of what he has experienced does fall under the banner of antisemitism, but he isn't too concerned about it. Particularly in the context of what it means to have come of age in the United States of 2020, a few insensitive comments aren't something he's too upset about. "There are people who have it way worse than me. It seems like every other day there's news about a Black person being killed or hurt or something. So yeah, I know my mom is nervous. But none of this is a big deal when you think about it like what it could be."

Bailey, whom we met in the introduction, currently studies in New York City and is originally from North Carolina. She grew up with a very small Jewish community, with only one or two other Jewish students in her grade from elementary school through high school. Her experience was not one of overt antisemitism but rather one of willful indifference. "Christianity was assumed, and there was no effort to even learn about other potential identities. So there would be tests scheduled during Rosh Hashanah and Yom Kippur and Passover. I was at the same school for fourteen years, and my mom raised these issues each time. You'd think these things could have been resolved, but there was a lack of acknowledgement." Bailey didn't make the decision about where she would go to college based on her Judaism, and when she got to her school, which has a very large and active Jewish population, not to mention the plethora of resources available to her in Manhattan, she quickly found herself overwhelmed. Without a clear place to call her own within the Jewish community, and unsure of whether or not she wanted to, Bailey got busy with her classes, her activism, and her writing.

Adolescence is a time when teens are engaged in the process of identity development. This involves the search for identity as adolescents try on different behaviors and appearances as part of the quest to discover who they are, and who they want to be.[5] With Jewish teens coming into their own as young adults, engaging with their multifaceted senses of self cannot be extracted from the backdrop of the changing state of the world and, particularly, from the prevalence of a newly emboldened antisemitic undertone in the United States. In 2019, the annual Audit of Antisemitic Incidents by the Anti-Defamation League (ADL) included 2,107 documented incidents throughout the United States.[6] This number not only represents a 12 percent increase from 2018 but also has the dubious honor of being the highest number on record since the ADL began tracking such incidents in 1979. With over 400 of these events occurring in K–12 school environments, it is clear that Generation Z adolescents are experiencing and facing antisemitism firsthand. During the time in their lives when they are exploring what aspects of their identities they want to embrace and lean into, if their Jewishness is a source of contention rather than pride, there is this natural concern: What will this mean for the Jewish future?

Cara, a high school junior from Illinois, is proud of her Judaism. She's a leader in a national Jewish youth movement and describes herself as confident when it comes to embracing every aspect of who she is. She says she's never experienced antisemitism in her public high school. I was relieved to hear that, grasping this pronouncement as evidence that things are okay, at least in the instance of this one teen, who is aware and would surely not stand for any slights to her Jewish identity. But as she continued, my sigh of relief caught in my throat. She said, "There've been incidents at my school, and things that people say, and jokes in passing that you always hear. It's about learning what to say in those situations, and for me personally, it's just casual and not meant to be hurtful. I'm definitely learning to figure out how to handle those situations and to figure out how to not bring the mood down or upset anyone, and how to behave in those conversations with non-Jews. I just don't want to make things awkward."

High school is a time when navigating peer culture is of paramount importance. Peer culture, a term originally coined by sociologist William Corsaro, refers to the set of "social rules" and behavioral routines that a peer group operates within.[7] If these often-unspoken rules and routines are breached, the group must undergo negotiations in order to stabilize the system of the group. While originally peer culture was observed in the context of young children, in the years of adolescence, the role of the peer group increases as teens become more autonomous and their informal interactions are less regulated by parents.[8] While in the context of

Generation Z, parents do play more of an active role in the lives of their teens than in any previous demographic cohort,[9] teens still find themselves eager to fit in with their peers, to find a social group, and to be accepted within it. Therefore, it is not surprising that from Cara's perspective, the most important thing was to not upset others and to keep things from becoming "awkward," even if that ultimately comes at the expense of standing up for herself in the face of antisemitism. Adam, who works for an international Israel education organization, described the paralysis that Jewish Generation Zers often feel. "Students are more afraid than they are educated. They don't really know what to do." Cara, together with her peers, personifies this struggle. Even when there's an understanding of something being wrong, and a feeling of discomfort, this does not naturally translate into action.

Ella is a high school senior in Los Angeles. While she is Jewish, she attends a private school that is nominally affiliated with Christianity, and she is one of few Jews in her school and social circles. She has heard classmates refer to Judaism as "watered-down Christianity" for years. As her Jewish identity has grown stronger through her affiliation with her youth group and her participation in Jewish leadership and internship programs, she has become more cognizant of antisemitic undertones in the words and behavior of some of her peers. "Sometimes I'll have a tinge that something is offensive, but if I'm not part of the group, I can't always point it out. I'll hear something and know that it's wrong but not always why or what to do about it." For many adolescents, the sense that as Jews it is incumbent on them to respond to antisemitic rhetoric can be intimidating and even prohibitive. While Ella has not always known how to respond to antisemitism in her circle of friends, as she's learned more, she has found herself rising to the challenge more and more. She recounted a story of going to a party earlier in her high school career. "Someone stood up on a table and said, 'I better not find out there are any Jewish kids here.'" As one of the only Jewish kids at the party, Ella could easily have chosen to keep silent or to leave. "I actually invited him to an Israel Club meeting. He didn't come, but I was proud of myself for extending the invite instead of just kind of laughing it off or ignoring it."

While it is understandable from the perspective of adolescent psychology that teens would prioritize remaining on the inside of their social group over raising concerns that they themselves may not understand, one can alternatively see Cara's and Ella's experiences less as incidents of underreported bullying and more as a commentary on American society as a whole. In the United States of the early 2020s, the dichotomy between the rise in hate speech and discrimination, on the one hand, and the culture of political correctness, on the other, has created a situation wherein Jewish students not only accept maltreatment as business as usual but actually believe it is incumbent on them to be concerned about the feelings of those who participate in these expressions of hate. For Cara's concern to be centered around how to not upset others when standing up to the antisemitism she experienced demonstrates a problem with the way that Jews and Jewish identity are understood within Generation Z.

Stephanie, a high school junior from New Jersey, is confident in standing proudly as a Jew. Her family regularly travels to Israel to visit her older sister, who moved there, and in between visits, Stephanie stays Jewishly connected through her leadership roles in her youth group and her summer camp. Her relationship with Judaism isn't defined by antisemitism but rather by a positive, communal version of Jewish life. "It's about the connection I have with people because of being Jewish. Being able to talk to someone and knowing we share the same culture and foods, and Jewish moms. . . . It's just so important to be part of the community, because it feels like you belong somewhere, and being Jewish gives me that."

According to James Gee's theory of identity, identity is defined as being recognized as a certain "kind of person" in a given context.[10] Gee's theory holds that social and cultural views of identity may take four different forms, including the affinity perspective, which is built by shared experiences as part of an affinity group. Joining this kind of group must be something that a person has chosen to do and feels a part of in order for the "A-identity" to be built. For Stephanie, being Jewish and affiliating with the Jewish community isn't just an inherited identity that she has passively accepted. It's something active that she has fully embraced and made her own. Historian Deborah Lipstadt, the author of the book *Antisemitism: Here and Now,* views this kind of active, self-actualized Judaism as a victory in and of itself. She tells the story of a man who failed to educate his children about Jewish traditions and culture but did succeed in instilling in them an intolerance of antisemitism.

Lipstadt writes, "Antisemitism has become the drummer to which his family's Jewish identity marches. They know of Jew as object, not subject. In other words, what is done *to* Jews becomes far more significant than what Jews *do*. . . . It leaves many Jews . . . aware of what to be *against* but not what to be *for*."[11] If the next generation of Jews is so focused on antisemitism, so alert to danger and hatred that they skip over the beauty and joy that comes from Jewish tradition, we have lost. When people say they're proud to be Jewish but have nothing of substance to back up that statement beyond they know that they're "supposed to be," the status quo is not sustainable. There is a limit to how much resilience can be fostered without the inspiration and strength that comes from an understanding that has both depth and breadth. When the foundational values that one ascribes to are more focused on minimizing the discomfort of others rather than standing up for oneself, there is a problem. At the same time, when one is expected to stand up without having a foundation as to why, there is a disconnect and an undue burden.

Jewish Generation Zers have been described as complex with regard to their developing Jewish identities. In the largest research study conducted on Jewish teens,[12] the guiding principle was "the vision that all Jewish teens in America will see their Jewish heritage as a source of wisdom, inspiration, and strength as they grow and discover their place in the world." This vision is one of proactive identity development, with positive associations, and is a concept that centers around building a strong sense of self as Jewish adolescents. While the by-product may be an ability to stand up to antisemitism, this is not the stated goal, and it is not a factor in any of the fourteen outcomes that define the ways Jewish education and experiences enable teens to flourish.

The teens who participated in the Generation Z Now study responded to queries about antisemitism in ways that mirror Cara's story above. While 45 percent affirmed that antisemitism is a problem for today's teens, they did not see it as a pressing personal problem. However, many teens reported behavior in which they felt negatively singled out for being Jewish. In one anecdote, a teen reported a boy making comments and jokes about her being Jewish, including, bluntly, "Shut up, you're Jewish." However, the teen did not feel this pattern of behavior warranted getting teachers involved, because she didn't want the "drama." In further clarification, the teen found the behavior annoying but did not feel as though she was being targeted. Nora, the college student from Connecticut (see the introduction), remembers experiences with antisemitism from as early as middle school. When some of her classmates went through what she referred to as the "white male teenage Nazi phase," giving Hitler salutes in the hallway, she wasn't sure how to relate to the experience. "It wasn't *at* me; it's hard for it *not* to be at me when I was the only Jewish person in the room."

Like too many of her peers, Nora did not receive the support that she wanted and needed from the authority figures she otherwise would have relied on. "It was very visible in the hallways and stuff, so it's hard to believe that no one noticed it. But no one talked to me or did anything about it, which feels even worse. At the moment, I didn't realize how wrong it was, but having it be recognized and talked about would have been helpful." Without the validation of the adults in her life, Nora was left floundering as to how to respond and wondering about the legitimacy of her feelings. Later on in high school, she again encountered a lack of support from the educators in her life. "I went to a very white, Christian school, and my teachers didn't know how to deal with anything different from that norm. They weren't open to my cultural knowledge. We read *Night*, by Elie Wiesel, and the teacher was pronouncing one of the names wrong. She wouldn't listen to me and wouldn't acknowledge that because of my identity, I could have knowledge and experiences that no one else did. I can't imagine what it must have been like being one of the few Black students, because being anything that was different was really hard."

Ella, the high schooler from Los Angeles whom we met earlier, succinctly summed up her feelings on how antisemitism fits into the greater backdrop of bullying, microaggressions, and targeting of minority groups. "It's not rocket science to understand when something is hurtful. Name calling is never OK, and it shouldn't be any different when it comes to antisemitism."

So where does this leave today's Jewish teens? How do we as a society reconcile the reality of antisemitism being on the rise with the next generation's reluctance to name it or allow it to define them? On the one hand, it can be seen as empowering. Perhaps it's indicative that Jewish Generation Zers are so proud, so strong, so confident in who they are that discrimination rolls off their backs. However, it can also be said to be demonstrative of a point where the teens are so lacking in identity markers that they don't recognize the signs, the reality. It's frightening that the go-to move is hesitating in the face of "drama" rather than advocating for themselves in the ways that their generation is otherwise wont to do. In American society today, one of the most-used phrases is "the new normal." The new normal is social distancing. The new normal is polarization. And for Jewish teens, perhaps the new normal is microaggressions, hard and soft antisemitism, and a reality of brushing off the discomfort that comes with the status quo. They are cognizant of how pervasive this reality has become. Bailey, the Manhattan-based college student, noted, "Antisemitism has entered into systems of power. The president of the United States is endorsing the Proud Boys.[13] But there's not much acknowledgment that it's happening." Ava from Los Angeles shared, "All hate crime is a big deal. I'm told that antisemitism isn't the biggest issue right now, but it's important. Antisemitism is an everyone problem."

As Generation Z comes into its own, this demographic cohort is poised to reshape the landscape of the United States politically, racially, and ethically. Forty-nine percent of Generation Zers identify as nonwhite. Ninety-eight percent own a smartphone, and 40 percent self-report to be addicted to said phones.[14] They are described as being pragmatic as compared to their more idealistic millennial counterparts. This manifests in their behavioral patterns as well as in their beliefs. During the 2018 midterm elections, a dramatic increase in youth voters was seen, as compared to the 2014 statistics.[15] However, 82 percent of youth say they're concerned about the values of the American people because of the results of the election, and 57 percent say they're losing faith in American democracy as a whole.[16] When more than half of the youngest, soon to be largest, demographic cohort in the country is actively concerned about the direction that the country is going in, it's cause for concern. There are many facets of American society that need to be reckoned with, and in the majority of cases it will be up to Generation Z to spearhead those processes. But at this moment, as this group comes into its own as influencers, change agents, and leaders, their pragmatism is being given one of its many tests. How does an educated, twenty-first-century society come to terms with the resurgence of history's oldest hatred?[17]

The Anti-Defamation League has produced what it calls the Pyramid of Hate, which can be found at https://www.adl.org/sites/default/files /documents/pyramid-of-hate.pdf. The pyramid illustrates the prevalence of bias, hate, and oppression in contemporary society. It is organized by escalating levels of attitudes and behavior that grow in complexity and extremism, with each level negatively impacting individuals, institutions, and society. It is meant to demonstrate that "when bias goes unchecked, it becomes 'normalized' and contributes to a pattern of accepting discrimination, hate, and injustice in society."[18] For Generation Z, as with other generations throughout history, ultimately getting to the top level, that of genocide, seems out of reach and unrealistic. And of course, that's a wonderful thing. But when the lowest levels are not taken seriously and are not met with intention, care, and concern, the pervasive hate present under the surface of a society continues to grow until ultimately it manifests in the most extreme of ways.

In the United States of the 2020s, nationwide data has shown that one in ten adults under forty cannot recall ever having heard the word "Holocaust."[19] The first fifty-state survey of Holocaust knowledge among millennials and Generation Z demonstrated shocking and frightening deficiencies. Sixty-three percent of those surveyed didn't know that six million Jews were murdered in the Holocaust, with more than half of the respondents saying that the death toll was less than two million. With nearly eleven thousand interviews conducted for this survey, it raises concerns about general ignorance and Holocaust denial. Eleven percent of respondents revealed that they believed Jews actually caused the Holocaust, with that number rising to 19 percent in New York—the state with the largest Jewish population in the United States.[20] These statistics are not simply concerning or disturbing. They are demonstrative of a new world that Generation Z has inherited, a world where things that could previously be taken for granted are no longer true. The very legitimacy of Jewish history and the collective Jewish experience have been called into question. Antisemitism is not just a question of hatred or of discrimination. It is a virus that has morphed in the United States of the 2020s into a multipronged monster, sucking knowledge, reason, and truth out of those who let it. While a lack of knowledge of the Holocaust is not inherently demonstrative of antisemitism, a culture that allows for the harmful spread of misinformation is responsible for fostering the resurgence of age-old tropes and stereotypes that allow the proliferation of antisemitic rhetoric to flourish.

Jonathan Woocher, whose predictive research on Jewish Generation Z was noted earlier, foresaw that youth culture for the postmillennial generation would lack a "hard edge of rebellion." Together with his colleagues, he wrote, "They will grow up in a Jewishly diverse world. They will take for granted being Jewish, and, perhaps as a result, feel less compelled to try to create their own. In this sense, they will be more conventional than the Generation Xers and Millennials who precede them, less eager to build new frameworks, though not necessarily more committed to existing ones." In many ways, Woocher was right. Generation Z Jews, by virtue of following the millennial generation, have less of a need to take on the task of building new institutions to meet the needs of a generation that sees the world in a new way, that has different definitions for what it means to connect, to gather, to belong. But without the knowledge of the uptick in antisemitism that was to come, Woocher was also wrong. Generation Z Jews are able to feel confident in being Jewish, to see a Jewish world full of color and diversity and a multiplicity of beliefs that is unprecedented. But against the backdrop of rising antisemitism, in a country torn apart by polarized politics, racial unrest, and generations of internalized anger spilling over in nearly every facet of society, it would be an error to say that Jewish Generation Zers have been spared the burden and responsibility of rebellion against the status quo. Their coming-of-age is marked by outspoken influencers, mobilizing activists, and a championing of the underdogs at this moment in history. In all of this, Jewish Generation Zers are no different from their counterparts from any faith tradition and indeed are all the more likely to take up causes as allies and activists.

For Generation Z, religion and the search for meaning are thought of differently than they were for previous generations. While human beings throughout history have grappled with questions of identity and how to find personal fulfillment in age-old traditions and institutions, the upending of previously assumed norms due to the digital revolution and the COVID-19 pandemic have fundamentally changed individual and collective relationships with religion across the board. Part of what needs to change in response to the new reality on the ground is the ways that things like religious affiliation and practice are measured. While typical surveys and focus groups may focus on perennial questions, such as belief in God or higher powers, when Generation Zers vote with their feet, their choices become clear: across religious denominations, teens may not identify as religious, but they are finding spirituality in arenas such as social justice and activism. According to Elizabeth Drescher, the author of *Choosing Our Religion: The Spiritual Lives of America's Nones*, teens are still searching for "social structures to express community cohesion and shared values and stories that create meaning."[21] For Jewish Generation Zers, finding these structures and outlets is a double challenge. As a minority in the United States and an emergent generation within the Jewish communal landscape, they are often pioneers, seeking new ways to tell their own stories and forge connections using the tools at their disposal, including social media, friend groups, and their external activities.

In Hebrew, the ancient and modern language of the Jewish people, there is no real word for "history." The colloquially used word is *historia*, which has been borrowed from English. Instead, the word that has traditionally been used is *zakhor*, or memory. In the collective lived experience of the Jewish people, time passing is not linear. Through rituals that call upon us to embody the lived experiences of our ancestors, and the cyclical nature of calendar and traditions alike, what has developed is a sense of collective memory and shared experience, regardless as to whether or not one was physically there. To have a sense of the scope of Jewish history, for me at least, is to live with ghosts—the ghosts of the people who should be here, the cousins who never had a chance to live, who in another time or place would have been here but for whom the march of history stopped before they had a chance to live. It's knowing that there are places, stories, secrets, that were left behind in another world, all for the promise of walking tall, proud, and Jewish, without any of those attributes being a contradiction to the others. The little girl who thought that all of the privilege she was born into would never be enough protection against the fate of the Jewish people in other times and places was a product of this reality. The lived experiences of the Generation Z Jewish teens, on the other hand, defy history. They are a product of their intersectional realities, and where this will lead them is the question that will shape the next generation.

NOTES

1. Bologna, C. (2019, November 8). What's the deal with Generation Alpha? HuffPost. Retrieved from https://www.huffpost.com/entry/genera tion-alpha-after-gen-z_l_5d420ef4e4b0aca341181574

2. Woocher, J., Belzer, T., Rozenfeld, M., & Woocher, M. (2008, March 1). Are we ready for the "post-Millennials"? Thoughts about tomorrow's Jewish students. Jewish Education Service of North America (JESNA).

3. Cohn, D., & Caumont, A. (2016, March 31). 10 demographic trends shaping the U.S. and the world in 2016. Pew Research Center. Retrieved from https://www.pewresearch.org/fact-tank/2016/03/31/10-demographic -trends-that-are-shaping-the-u-s-and-the-world

4. Twenge, J. M. (2017). *iGen: Why today's super-connected kids are growing up less rebellious, more tolerant, less happy and completely unprepared for adulthood—and what that means for the rest of us.* New York: Atria Books.

5. Strasburger, V. C., Wilson, B. J., & Jordan, A. B. (2014). Children and adolescents: Unique audiences. In *Children, adolescents, and the media* (pp. 11–19). Los Angeles: SAGE.

6. Anti-Defamation League. "Audit of Antisemitic Incidents, 2019." Retrieved from https://www.adl.org/audit2019

7. Corsaro, W. A. (1994). Discussion, debate, and friendship: Peer discourse in nursery schools in the United States and Italy. *Sociology of Education, 67,* 1–26.

8. Coleman, J. S. (1961). *The adolescent society: The social life of the teenager and its impact on education.* New York: Free Press of Glencoe.

9. Twenge, *iGen.*

10. Gee, J. P. (2000). Identity as an analytic lens for research in education. *Review of Research in Education, 25,* 99–125.

11. Lipstadt, D. E. (2019). *Antisemitism: Here and now.* New York: Schocken Books.

12. Levites, A., & Sayfan, L. (2019). *GenZ now: Understanding and connecting with today's Jewish teens.* The Jewish Education Project and Rosov Consulting.

13. Hesson, T., & Cooke, K. (2020, September 30). Explainer: President Trump asked the Proud Boys to "stand by." Who are they? Reuters. Retrieved from https://www.reuters.com/article/us-usa-election-extremists-explainer/explainer-president-trump-asked-the-proud-boys-to-stand-by-who-are-they-idUSKBN26L3Q1

14. Desjardins, J. (2019, February 14). Meet Generation Z: The newest members of the workforce. *Visual Capitalist.* Retrieved from https://www.visualcapitalist.com/meet-generation-z-the-newest-member-to-the-workforce

15. Center for Information & Research on Civic Learning and Engagement (2019, May 30). 28% of young people voted in 2018. CIRCLE: Center for Information & Research on Civic Learning and Engagement. Retrieved from https://circle.tufts.edu/latest-research/28-young-people-voted-2018

16. Center for Information & Research on Civic Learning and Engagement (2019, April 17). Youth voting rose in 2018 despite concerns about American democracy. CIRCLE: Center for Information & Research on Civic Learning and Engagement. Retrieved from https://circle.tufts.edu/latest-research/youth-voting-rose-2018-despite-concerns-about-american-democracy

17. Jacoby, J. (2009, March 11). History's oldest hatred. Boston.com. Retrieved from http://archive.boston.com/bostonglobe/editorial_opinion/oped/articles/2009/03/11/historys_oldest_hatred

18. Anti-Defamation League (n.d.). Pyramid of hate. Anti-Defamation League. Retrieved from https://www.adl.org/media/12060/download

19. Ramgopal, K. (2020, September 16). Survey finds "shocking" lack of Holocaust knowledge among millennials and Gen Z. NBC News. Retrieved from https://www.nbcnews.com/news/world/survey-finds-shocking-lack-holocaust-knowledge-among-millennials-gen-z-n1240031

20. Claims Conference (2020, September 16). First-ever 50-state survey on Holocaust knowledge of American millennials and Gen Z reveals shocking results. Retrieved from http://www.claimscon.org/millennial-study.

21. Jaradat, M. (2020, September 13). Gen Z's looking for religion. You'd be surprised where they find it. *Deseret News*. Retrieved from https://www.deseret.com/indepth/2020/9/13/21428404/gen-z-religion-spirituality-social-justice-black-lives-matter-parents-family-pandemic

TWO

Never Again: The Burden of the Last Generation to Meet Holocaust Survivors

If understanding is impossible, knowing is imperative, because what happened could happen again.

—Primo Levi, *The Reawakening*

As a child, a central pillar of my Jewish upbringing was the weekly experience of Shabbat services in my family's synagogue. I was one of few children in attendance. The majority of congregants were not interested in battling with their offspring about the merits of Saturday morning prayers as opposed to soccer or slumber parties or any of the other hallmarks of our suburban middle-class community. Those other children who did come were often found jumping on the couch in the women's bathroom or running races down the hallways. I, on the other hand, could reliably be found in the third row on the left, near my father, following the service and soaking in the melodies of the Hebrew prayers. You could say I was pious or that I was devout, but the most accurate descriptor would be that I was a highly cerebral and slightly uncool child, far more comfortable and at ease in the company of adults than in the company of my peers. This was never truer than at the kiddush luncheon following the weekly service. Instead of joining the group at the self-proclaimed kids' table or grabbing a brownie and continuing the hallway races, I could be counted on to make my way to the seat nearest to an elegant senior citizen named Charlotte.

Charlotte spoke with a soft voice and a rolling accent. She dressed in beautifully tailored suits and smelled like perfume. She had her own grandchildren, a few years older than me, but since they never came to services, I was able to bask in her attention. At first, I was drawn to her sparkling jewelry and her smile. I would sit next to her and chatter, telling her about my art classes and what I was reading. But soon I found that her stories were the ones far more worth listening to. I don't remember the first time I heard her say the words that I'd seen written in books. Words like Auschwitz. Bergen Belsen. Mengele. But soon I began to understand. Charlotte was a link between the history that I read about, which seemed far enough away to not be real, and my very real life. She had been there for all of it. As a teenager, she survived the concentration camps. She lost her family but found love after the war. She immigrated to the United States with her husband and young baby, as her home of Czechoslovakia was not a place she was able to return to. Charlotte had the ubiquitous blue numbers tattooed on her skin under the sleeves of her elegant Shabbat clothes. I would sit silently, drinking in her words, knowing that I could never understand but desperately wanting to know.

Growing up in a Jewish community in the New York suburbs, Charlotte was not the only Holocaust survivor in my life. My own grandmother had been a refugee, fleeing Berlin as a child with her parents. I know the stories of her early days with more precision than I can recall some of my own. I know that my great-grandfather, Markus Adler, was a furrier from Radymno, Poland, who had his own store in Berlin. I know that one day after Hitler came to power, his non-Jewish employee came into the store and punched my great-grandmother Sophie in the face, announcing that the store was now his. I know the family ran, crisscrossing Europe under the growing specter of Nazism until they were able to secure passage to New York thanks to a relative vouching for them. I know that as a young child, my grandmother was chased on her bicycle once the other children realized she was a Jew, and she internalized the fear of having blown her family's cover. I never learned how to ride a bike. I don't know if any part of my child's psyche connected Grandma's story with my own reluctance to move beyond training wheels, but looking back I can't help but see the link.

Knowing is perhaps the wrong word. I wasn't just aware of these realities. I internalized them before I was ready. Grandma's stories, Charlotte's stories, and the stories from the genre of youth Holocaust literature that I couldn't get enough of mixed in my mind before I could understand that time is linear and these events were in the past. There were questions I couldn't ask, and I relied on classics like *Number the Stars* and *The Devil's Arithmetic* to fill in the blanks. The Holocaust is a never-ending subject, and I absorbed more than I could. Indeed, an iconic story of my childhood is that one of the few times I got in trouble, it was because I was reading a book about the twins that Nazi scientist Josef Mengele experimented on in Auschwitz. My mother confiscated the book, concerned that it was upsetting me and making me lash out at my siblings. She hid it between the beach towels in the hall closet, where it still remains nearly twenty years later. I never finished the book. But I never forgot the stories either.

In the Jewish tradition, we are taught the story of the Amalekites, which is found throughout the Torah. The nation of Amalek was an enemy of the Israelite people. Understood to be descendants of Esau, and therefore natural rivals of the emergent Israelite nation, their first encounter is chronicled in the book of Exodus. In Exodus 17, as the Israelites wander in the desert following the exodus from Egypt, Amalek attacks the weakened people. The ensuing battle is a massacre, and in its wake, the Israelite people are left with a perplexing commandment: remember to forget. It is written: Then the Lord said to Moses, "Inscribe this in a document as a reminder, and read it aloud to Joshua: I will utterly blot out the memory of Amalek from under heaven" (Exodus 17:14)! In this verse, the Israelite people are given the order to remember to forget. They're tasked with blotting out the memory of their attackers. But they are simultaneously prohibited from forgetting their actions and this painful, bloody interlude in the collective history of the people.

The Amalekites have become synonymous with enemies that the Jewish people have faced over time, ensuring that their memory was never fully wiped out. But from biblical times to the twentieth century, the commandment following an assault on the Jewish people changed. Instead of remembering to forget, the watchword became the now-iconic "Never Again."

Never Again is the core of modern Holocaust education and commemoration. Its origins as a catchphrase are thought to have originated in a 1927 poem by Yitzhak Lamdan, a Ukrainian-born writer who moved to Mandatory Palestine as a youth. His epic poem, "Masada: A Historical Epic," depicted the Jewish struggle for survival in a world of enemies and includes the line, "Never again shall Masada fall!"[1] With this source immediately linking the phrase with a saga centered around a Jewish minority standing up to the threats against it, the groundwork was inherently laid for "Never Again" to become the Holocaust's legacy. The phrase was first associated with the Holocaust itself in its most immediate aftermath, when survivors of the Buchenwald concentration camp displayed the phrase on homemade signs after their liberation.[2]

According to scholars Diana Popescu and Tanja Schult, the original use of "Never Again" in Buchenwald had two distinctive meanings. The phrase was used by political prisoners, who said "Never again" in the context of their fight against fascism, as well as by Jewish survivors, whose focus was to never *forget* the destruction of their families and communities. However, the scholars say that in the subsequent years, the distinction was blurred for a more universalist Holocaust lesson. Over time, the phrase has evolved from being associated specifically and exclusively with the Holocaust and has been applied to other genocides,[3] ethnic cleansings, and more recently, anti-gun violence groups in the aftermath of the shooting at Marjorie Stoneman Douglas High School.[4] Holocaust survivor, writer, and leading thinker Elie Wiesel reflected on the now-iconic phrase: "Never again becomes more than a slogan: It's a prayer, a promise, a vow."[5] Never Again is a touchstone for many who work in the space of Holocaust education, as it is for their learners and alumni. Jewish Generation Zers have been raised with this ethos, and many have internalized the rallying cry as a core part of their Jewish identities. According to the Pew Research Center's 2013 report, 73 percent of American Jews (not accounting for age) said that remembering the Holocaust is an essential part of what it means to be Jewish.[6] This was the most-received response, outranking leading an ethical/moral life, caring about Israel, eating traditional Jewish foods, and having a good sense of humor, among other choices. This trend continued in the 2020 report, in which it was found that 76 percent of American Jews listed remembering this Holocaust as one of the five most essential factors in their Judaism.[7] It is clear that the outsized role of the Holocaust in the contemporary Jewish psyche continues, and as Generation Z moves into the forefront of American Jewish life, they will have to grapple with this reality, while watching as the generation of survivors dies out at a rapid pace.

The emphasis on the Holocaust is not just worth noting for its influence inside the Jewish community. It is being co-opted, particularly by the alt-right, who have coined the term "six gorillion," a play on the six million Jews who were slaughtered by the Nazis. Six gorillion first entered into alt-right parlance in 2013 and has increased in its dubious popularity since then.[8] This mocking phrase is meant to convey the impression that the

Jewish people have exaggerated the number of people who actually died in the Holocaust. While for some, it's easy to shrug off this kind of anti-semitism and deliberate misinformation campaign, others see these trends as ominous warning signs. The delegitimization of the Holocaust, coupled with those who are simply uninformed about its facts due to lack of education and access, has the power to lead to a rewriting of history as the loss of survivors changes the story that is being told.

For Generation Z, the recognition of the responsibility that comes with being the final generation that will be able to speak directly to Holocaust survivors and learn their stories firsthand has inspired a plethora of educational opportunities, all geared toward the collective goal of providing connection, moral education, and an understanding of what happened during the Holocaust, as well as the importance of ensuring it will never happen again. This has taken on a variety of formats, with each educator bringing a different pedagogy meant to align with their goals and values when it comes to introducing the Holocaust to new generations.

Adina Baseman Sharfstein is a veteran educator in Broward County, Florida. A teacher in the elementary school system and in the district's gifted program, she has spent thirty years teaching young learners reading, writing, and the Holocaust. While there are a variety of perspectives about when young students are developmentally prepared to take on the complex, challenging subject of the Holocaust, the recommendations of the United States Holocaust Museum are that teaching individual eyewitness accounts of the Holocaust, as well as placing its events into their historical context, is achievable for students in grades six and above. While elementary schoolers are able to empathize with individual accounts of the Holocaust, they have difficulty processing them as historical data points.[9]

Adina places the Holocaust into the context of human rights for her young learners. By teaching a diverse population, including both Jewish and non-Jewish students, she is able to provide grounding and nuance in her explorations of Holocaust narratives. And as an educator, she feels a deep sense of responsibility in opening the eyes of her students to the realities of the past and the present. "Courageous conversations have to start in the classroom, because they won't always start at home. Even though parents are the biggest influences, we don't tap enough into the role of teachers in the classroom. Understanding LGBTQ rights, anti-racism, antisemitism—it all starts in the classroom." When the Holocaust is taught to the youngest of students, it lays the groundwork for emerging world-views that are informed by empathy, respect, and the importance of doing the right thing. While Adina does not seek to romanticize the heroes of the Holocaust by overemphasizing their role as compared to the many who stayed silent or who worked to perpetuate the atrocities that were committed, she does strike a balance that honors the ability of individuals to do the right thing and make an impact through their actions.

Sally is a drama therapist who directs a program called Witness Theater at an Orthodox high school. Originally an Israeli program, Witness Theater premiered in the United States in the early 2000s. Its ethos combines Holocaust education, creative arts, and storytelling. Practically, it's a yearlong program wherein high school students and Holocaust survivors come together for a process known as embodied storytelling. The students meet with the survivors and learn their stories firsthand before beginning the transformation of the stories into a theatrical production. "It's a literal stepping into their shoes and taking on their stories. Once you physicalize someone's story, you're part of it. First, you're someone's witness, and then you're their storyteller. It's a passing on of the role of witness." At this juncture in history, with fewer than four hundred thousand Holocaust survivors still living,[10] there is an urgency in creating as many young witnesses as possible.

Building relationships with survivors can be transformative for members of both generations. Jess, a twenty-something New Jersey native who works as a social worker, identifies deeply with being a "3G": a third-generation descendant of a Holocaust survivor. Her grandmother is a Holocaust survivor, and she has internalized the responsibility of not letting her story be forgotten. "It's a big role to pass on the tradition and to make sure her story is known. I feel drawn to making something of myself and not letting what she went through be for nothing." This experience, of feeling called or committed to ensuring that their lives are intentionally lived, is common among descendants of survivors in both the second and third generations. As Generation Zers, many of whom are fourth-generation survivors or who do not have a familial connection to the Holocaust, take the mantle of passing on the stories, this sense of personal responsibility may be what carries them forward.

Deborah Fripp is a Holocaust educator in Texas whose pedagogy is guided by a core question. Instead of asking what it was like to die in the Holocaust, she states, we need to ask, What was it like to live? Like Sally, she uses storytelling and creative theater as vehicles for accessing the legacy of the Holocaust. Specifically, she challenges her learners to explore the takeaways from the Holocaust that can be applied to their own lives, challenges fellow educators to figure out "how to teach the Holocaust without involving PTSD," and challenges herself to reinvent what Holocaust education looks like for Generation Z. "We need to create a structure that doesn't rely on survivors but that can speak to survivors and bring their lessons to life. That way we can think about what we can learn and how we as a people can move forward."

Deborah's answer to these various challenges has been to create mechanisms through which to ritualize the act of remembering the Holocaust. The way she sees things, "Our job isn't to teach kids the history of the Holocaust. They're going to learn it elsewhere—in regular school, in pop culture, or somewhere. Our job is to give them the visceral sense of 'this is *my* story and I want to be part of this story that previous generations accessed from interacting with survivors, and internalizing what it means to be important to them because you're the continuation of the story.'" In order to achieve this elusive goal of taking ownership of the story of the Holocaust and internalizing its messages in order to carry them forward, Deborah has focused on what it means to create rituals that ensure continuity. She looked at other pivotal moments in the collective Jewish story and took note of which ones are remembered as well as which ones have faded into the forgotten memories of history.

"We remember the Exodus [from Egypt] without survivors because we've ritualized it [in the Passover seder].[11] We *don't* remember the expulsion from Spain in 1492.[12] So we need to stop thinking about [the Holocaust] traumatically and to start thinking about what lessons we can learn from it. The seder doesn't spend a lot of time talking about the trauma of slavery and how people were killed. It focuses on what we should learn from the experience. That's the key." While Deborah does not discount the power of survivor testimony, and the central role that those directly impacted by the Holocaust have had on ensuring the continuation of its legacy for future generations, as an educator in a small Jewish community, she has never had the ready access to survivors that many of her colleagues in other places have enjoyed. By virtue of these circumstances, she has worked to pioneer models of Holocaust education that are not contingent on survivors in order to have a lasting and transformative impact. She believes that "it's one thing to hear a survivor talk. It's another thing to tell that story and to tell it as if it's your own."

Rob was a participant in immersive Holocaust education programs. He grew up in an interfaith household with a Jewish mother and a non-Jewish father. From early childhood, he was given a strong sense of his Jewish identity, despite growing up in a largely non-Jewish context. He holds the status of being the only Jew in his school in Texas and has often felt that no one understood him or his needs. He argued with school administration, because not being in school for Jewish holidays was listed as an unexcused absence. His direct encounters with antisemitism began in middle school. "People thought I was weird because I was Jewish. There was one kid who would give the Nazi salute every time I walked by him in the hallway. I told the teachers, but he never got into any kind of trouble."

Rob has never had the opportunity to meet a Holocaust survivor in person. But he was able to see films of survivor testimonies and internalized the messages of resilience in the face of evil and hatred, which ultimately bolstered his resolve to express his Judaism against an ever-encroaching cloud of antisemitism. He remembers the Unite the Right rally in Charlottesville in 2017 that was marked by the resounding cry "Jews will not replace us."[13] Rob, who is active in his synagogue, wondered, Could that happen here? Ultimately, his synagogue was hit by a physical manifestation of antisemitism. Its playground was tagged with antisemitic graffiti, putting Rob, who saw it while supervising a group of younger students, in the position of having to shield them from an awareness of the hatred that faced them, all the while internalizing it himself. Regardless of his legitimate, all-too-grounded fears, Rob continues to be strong in his own Jewish identity. He aspires to attend a college with a robust Jewish life and to intentionally live Jewishly throughout his life. "If we hide in the shadows, it just encourages antisemitism."

Melinda's father was a survivor of Dachau. He was the sole member of his family to live through the war. While he died before Melinda's daughter, a young Generation Zer, was born, the emotional inheritance of the Holocaust runs deep within their family. Melinda describes her own role as the bridge between the memory of what happened to her father and family and her child. "There's a massive intellectual and emotional onus on me to pass that legacy along. The Holocaust isn't around every corner in our lives today, but we can't say that it isn't possible. Because it is, and it happened to our family. We need to be on guard for ourselves and also for other communities that could be at risk for it happening. It's hopefully a value of decent human beings, but it also feels like a particular imperative rooted in our family history."

Mara, the freshman at the State University of New York at Binghamton, grew up in an active Jewish family, with a background that involved attending Jewish day schools, summer camps, and involvement in her youth group. She is active in both Jewish and progressive circles and sees the two as aligned in her life. "When I'm in non-Jewish spaces, particularly political or activism spaces, my Judaism is the frame through which I see those places, and it's why I choose to be there." Mara has grown up and been educated to be aware of the Holocaust as well as the personal and collective responsibility of ensuring that its legacy is never forgotten. However, like many of her peers, her understandings and beliefs regarding that legacy differ from those of previous generations.

In 2018, historian Waitman Wade Beorn wrote in the *Washington Post* that the detention centers on the border between the United States and Mexico were concentration camps. In using this term that is deeply connected to the Holocaust, this scholar of Holocaust and genocide studies meaningfully compared the conditions between the detention centers and Camp de Rivesaltes, a French concentration camp, which was different from a death camp such as the more commonly known Auschwitz, Bergen Belsen, or Treblinka. The criteria that Beorn used as the basis for this comparison was that the Camp de Rivesaltes was "a temporary, insufficiently conceived facility designed to prevent foreigners from entering the country," a descriptor that he said also applied to the detention centers.[14] This statement was met with a tremendous amount of backlash from many within the Jewish community, particularly after other scholars and thought leaders began to use the term.[15]

The controversy around using the phrase "concentration camps" came from both individuals and organizations. In 2019, then-freshman congresswoman Alexandria Ocasio-Cortez tweeted, "This [Trump] administration has established concentration camps on the southern border of the United States for immigrants, where they are being brutalized with dehumanizing conditions and dying." Groups from the Anti-Defamation League to the Simon Wiesenthal Center to noted individuals, including Professor Deborah Lipstadt, a noted expert on antisemitism, pushed back against the use of the term "concentration camp" while decrying the humanitarian conditions in the border detention facilities.[16] Leading Conservative Jewish Rabbi David Wolpe, for example, said on the topic of Representative Ocasio-Cortez's words: "It is baffling why someone would choose a term to condemn cruelty that is guaranteed to make the argument about the term and not about the policy. Analogies that evoke the Holocaust are, with the rarest exceptions, presumptively offensive and unwise."

At the same time, the rabbi was critical of the detention centers themselves. "It's appalling and it's unthinkable for the United States to treat people—whether they're admitted or not to the country—in such a manner, and all of us should be better than that. If you can't unite as a country to prevent the suffering of children then we're in just abominable and disgraceful shape."

While many in the American Jewish establishment, particularly of older generations, bristled at the perceived cheapening or watering down of Holocaust terminology by applying it to other historical moments, many Generation Zers did not see the problem. Indeed, they saw the Holocaust as the impetus for their own activism related to the situation at the U.S.-Mexico border. An activist organization called Never Again Action noted, "As Jews, we've been taught to never let anything like the Holocaust happen again. Now, with children detained in unacceptable conditions, ICE raids targeting our communities, and people dying at the border while seeking safety in the U.S., we are seeing the signs of a mass atrocity. We refuse to wait and see what happens next."[17]

SUNY freshman Mara has had a Holocaust education that instilled in her a great respect for the magnitude of the Holocaust in history but has also empowered her to use its legacy to create change. "I get confused about other people's sensitivities regarding Holocaust imagery. When people said you can't call the detention facilities on the southern border a concentration camp, well, why not? If that's what it takes to get my parents, my aunts, or my grandparents to listen to what's going on, why not? I think that's a fine way to use our history." She acknowledged that others take significant issue with this school of thought. "People say, 'Well, my ancestors died in concentration camps, and you're using that imagery to talk about kids in a dirty facility? And I'm like, they're dead, they don't know what I'm saying, and if we can use this to advance the cause of justice, that's a good thing."

Alyssa Weinstein-Sears, a Holocaust educator from Texas, agreed. In her work with Generation Zers, as well as with learners of all ages, she has found some universal truths. "You cannot compare pain. Victims are victims, survivors are survivors, and trauma is trauma." She commends young Jews who have used the Holocaust as an inspiration in advancing modern social justice causes. After all, she says, "There's a switch where your history has to become your advocacy."

Claire Sarnowski is a high school student from Oregon. She does not fit the typical profile for this book. She's not Jewish, and on paper, she has no direct connection to the Holocaust. But her activism and early commitment to creating change thrust her to the forefront of Oregon's Holocaust Education Bill, SB 664. As of 2021, only seventeen states require any kind of

Holocaust education for secondary school students.[18] An additional two states encourage, while not requiring, the inclusion of the Holocaust in the curriculum taught to their students. It is understood that knowledge of the details of the Holocaust is currently at an all-time low,[19] and there have been increasing efforts by Jewish communities and allies nationwide to ensure that Holocaust education becomes a meaningful part of the academic careers of adolescents. For Claire, advocating for mandatory Holocaust education in Oregon was a pinnacle moment in a lifetime of activism.

When Claire was three years old, her mother held a volunteer role as a patient advocate for individuals with multiple sclerosis. Claire went with her mother to conferences relating to the treatment and search for a cure for the disease, and, as a caring and precocious toddler, decided that she wanted to do something to help. Upon returning home to Oregon, Claire began raising money for the MS walk, and she was determined to do it all by herself. She went door to door, with parental chaperones, but was facilitated largely by her own drive. At the age of three, she raised over $1,000 from her efforts. This staggering success was just the beginning of a lifetime of activism. Last year, she raised over $9,000 through her efforts, with goals to continue growing exponentially in the coming years. In keeping with her precocious nature and multifaceted interests, Claire began reading about the Holocaust as an elementary schooler. The topic was introduced by her mother, who had the opportunity to visit the Dachau concentration camp and was deeply impacted by the experience.

When Claire was in fourth grade, her aunt, an educator, invited her to hear a Holocaust survivor speak for the first time. It was then that Claire met Alter Weiner, a survivor and educator who spent years sharing his story of survival with the Oregon community.[20] She and Alter connected and began a friendship that would last until his death. When speaking about her relationship with Alter, Claire emphasized its mutual nature. "People used to say to me, 'it's so great you have him as a grandpa figure.' But he wasn't a grandparent to me. He was a friend. We clicked, and it felt so natural. He was always so easy to talk to." Claire and Alter remained in each other's orbits for years, until her home community experienced its own uptick in antisemitic activity. Posters were hung in the local high school cafeteria with images of Jewish people being pushed into crematoria with the caption "EZ Bake Oven." Swastika graffiti appeared on lockers and notebooks. The uptick in antisemitism was a stream of a larger epidemic of intolerance and racism as a whole, which included a noose being drawn on a desk and notes containing racial slurs being delivered to the handful of Black students. As the school district grappled with what to do, one answer came in the form of Alter. By bringing him in to share his story of survival and overcoming hate, the school created a lasting impact on many students. According to Claire, people became more careful about what they said and how they treated one another.

Alter shared with Claire his desire to ensure that all Oregonians have the opportunity to be exposed to Holocaust education so that the impact of its stories and legacy could be felt exponentially. Inspired by Alter and the activism that her peers were engaging in at the time in Parkland, Florida,[21] Claire got to work. This time, the precocious young activist faced a more uphill battle than she had when raising money to find a cure for MS. "People told me I was too young [to advocate for the bill], and to go back to the classroom." And it wasn't just naysayers questioning Claire's age whom she had to contend with. "There were Holocaust deniers protesting, who compared pictures of the death camps to child pornography." Claire acknowledges that her age has made people underestimate her, but she counters it with her innately strong will. "I'll always try. If it takes me ten minutes or ten years, I'll keep trying and trying."

In July 2019, Senate Bill 665 was signed into law in Oregon, with Governor Kate Brown including the following in her prepared remarks: "Senate Bill 665 mandates our schools to teach Oregon's students about these scars of history so that each generation can prevent such actions from ever happening again." Governor Brown thanked Claire for her leadership in pushing the bill forward and setting into motion a new reality wherein Oregon's children will be given the opportunity to engage with the Holocaust's reality as well as its legacy. For Claire, it was the culmination of a quest that she began in partnership with Alter and finished in his memory. Claire credits Alter, and the transformative relationship she built with him, for shaping her efforts. "The best tool any of us have is the power of knowledge and education. The best thing we can do is to channel our efforts into acknowledging that our education shows now only the atrocities but also the bravery and the legacy of the survivors. This history can never be forgotten." While Claire's relationship with the Holocaust predated Alter, and her encounters with its legacy continue after his death, it is the relationship that inspired her to action, and the endurance of a personal narrative that bridged the generations.

Adina Baseman Sharfstein, the elementary school teacher from Broward County, Florida, takes an alternative view on the role of Holocaust survivors telling their stories to Generation Zers. "A survivor should never be the way students learn about the Holocaust. It is not the survivor's job to teach the Holocaust. It is only their wish to share their stories." This perspective has set Adina, and her students, up for success in a world that sees survivors aging, becoming infirm, and ultimately dying. The COVID-19 pandemic has only hastened this reality, putting educators in the position of immediately needing to pivot and figure out how to teach the Holocaust in a way that is not contingent on the survivors being present to share their stories. It is a known fact that hearing stories is more transformative, and leaves more of a lasting impact, than facts alone.[22] Recognizing that as Holocaust education evolves, the need to tell its stories in new ways that leave lasting impressions for students will only grow in importance, educators have begun to shift their mindsets and best practices. Adam, who works with high schoolers throughout the Midwest, summed up his mission in educating students about the Holocaust and about antisemitism more broadly defined. "The key is finding ways to make students feel accountable for passing on the stories." Hannah, a marketing professional, has chosen to share the story of her survivor grandfather using social media. She prioritizes exploring his legacy beyond the years of the war. "My grandfather's story isn't defined by concentration camps. It's defined by going *through* the concentration camps and overcoming that." With the face of Holocaust education shifting, there's an emerging trend of placing the Holocaust into a larger global and historical context of genocide and hate, which is being spurred by educators who approach the topic with a new lens.

"I attribute ninety-eight percent of my success as a Holocaust and genocide educator to the fact that I started when I was under thirty. There is a disconnect from survivors. Survivor testimony can be great, but the question is, How can you get kids to engage with it when it feels far away, or irrelevant?" Alyssa Weinstein-Sears teaches middle school students in a public school setting as well as high schoolers in Jewish supplementary schools. Her passion for sharing the legacy of the Holocaust with learners from a variety of backgrounds shines through. She recognizes the pivot point that Holocaust education is at and the importance of it continuing to be relevant and applicable. "Survivor talks on Yom HaShoah [Holocaust Remembrance Day] are gone. We're past that; that's not what Holocaust education is anymore. It's having a face, and saying I'm here to teach you and to learn from you."

Alyssa's experience in teaching the Holocaust is not limited to Jewish students. In a world where two-thirds of American millennials don't know what Auschwitz is,[23] ensuring that Generation Z turns the tide and fulfills the commandment to never forget has become all the more pressing. According to a 2020 Pew study on religious knowledge, it was found that education, visiting a Holocaust museum, and knowing a Jewish person are three factors strongly linked with Holocaust knowledge.[24] When given four multiple-choice questions about the Holocaust, American adults who had never been to a Holocaust museum or memorial were able to answer 2 of the questions correctly, whereas those who had (27% of all respondents) were able to answer 2.9 questions accurately. Similarly, those who did not know anyone Jewish answered one fewer question correctly than those who did, for an average of 1.5 correct answers for those who didn't know any Jews as compared to 2.6 for those who did. For reference, the questions asked were:

1. When did the Holocaust happen? (Answer options: 1890–1910, 1910–1930, **1930–1950**, 1950–1970)

2. What were Nazi-created ghettos? (Answer options: Places where Jews were killed in gas chambers, factories where Nazis forced their political opponents to work, **parts of a city/town where Jews were forced to live**, housing developments for poor Nazis)

3. In total, about how many Jews were killed in the Holocaust? (Answer options: Less than 1 million, approximately 3 million, **approximately 6 million**, more than 12 million)

4. Which best describes how Adolf Hitler became chancellor of Germany? (Answer options: Violently overthrowing the German government, hereditary succession, agreements with neighboring countries, **a democratic political process**)

The Pew study asked the same questions of teens ages thirteen through seventeen. The teens' levels of Holocaust knowledge were similar to those of adults without postsecondary education. While more than half (57%) knew when the Holocaust occurred and what Nazi-created ghettos were (53%), less than half knew how many Jews were killed during the Holocaust (38%) and how Hitler became the chancellor of Germany (33%).[25] As this generation comes of age, the lack of knowledge about key details of the Holocaust, including things as fundamental as the number of Jews who were killed, can be seen as laying the groundwork for further misconceptions, falsehoods, and even corruptions of its legacy. In a world where Facebook had to take the measure of specifically banning Holocaust denial posts and content,[26] a lack of basic Holocaust education has the potential to spiral into distortions that shape beliefs, policies, and behaviors. It's this drive to provide an education that informs behaviors that inspires Alyssa. "I tell my students, I'm not expecting you to go out and stop a genocide. I expect you to use what you know about the Holocaust and the steps that got us to this horrible point to look at what's going on in Ethiopia, or in Sudan, to bring it up, and to use your social media outlets and say, 'This is a problem and because I'm Jewish, I know this is a problem and I'm going to stand up for the people in Ethiopia or Darfur or China, and I'm going to call this out.' So don't file this knowledge away and think it's only relevant to Jewish people. Find your social action moment and use this, and let it be the basis for saying 'I'm not going to be a voice that was silent, because when our people needed someone to stand up, no one did. So I'm not going to be silent when others need it.'"

When it comes to the teaching of the Holocaust to Generation Z, there are certain new norms that are already reshaping Holocaust education in the twenty-first century. For the majority of the period between the Holocaust itself and today, there has been an assumed norm of not using Holocaust imagery to further conversations on other topics.[27] One would be roundly reprimanded for calling someone they didn't like a Nazi or referring to a prison as a concentration camp. There was a shared understanding, albeit implicitly in most cases, that the Holocaust was so massive, so tragic, so removed from any modern injustice, that to use the wording associated with it was to somehow cheapen it and sensationalize the crisis du jour. However, particularly in the years since the election of President Donald Trump, this has changed.

In late 2018, Holocaust historian Dr. Edna Friedberg wrote, "Nazis seem to be everywhere these days. I don't mean self-proclaimed neo-Nazis. I'm talking about folks being labeled as Nazis, Hitler, Gestapo, Goering—take your pick—by their political opponents. American politicians from across the ideological spectrum, influential media figures and ordinary people on social media casually use Holocaust terminology to bash anyone or any policy with which they disagree. The takedown is so common that it's even earned its own term, reductio ad Hitlerum."

A generation ago, part of the burden of Holocaust educators would be to explain to students why they should not stand for anything else being compared to the tragedy of the Holocaust. But now, some educators are proactively placing the Holocaust into a larger arc of history and are intentionally using Holocaust terminology to give meaning to new global events. Alyssa Weinstein-Sears reflected on her efforts to help the teenagers she teaches enter into an emotional and empathetic space that allows them to meaningfully engage with the content of the past and the present. "When I say, 'Let's talk about extermination,' it's not just gas chambers. It's slave labor. We can make a connection to slavery, and to border camps, because concentration camps don't just mean gas chambers and crematoria. It means a prison camp where everyone is from the same group of people."

The Holocaust is a constant specter, in many ways increasing in relevance with the passage of time rather than fading into the pages of textbooks and black-and-white photos. It can inspire action in honor of the memory of the dead and commitments and allyship to the mission statement of Never Again. But it can also be corrupted and used for the ongoing spreading and fostering of hate. Rebecca, a college student from Texas, describes herself as a Bible Belt–raised Reform Jew/atheist. She's bold and proud of her status as a Jew, an activist, and a member of the LGBTQI community. Her brushes with antisemitism began in elementary school, when people told her she was going to go to hell for not believing in Jesus. This carried forward to high school, where she was regularly greeted with a Hitler salute. And at the onset of the Trump administration, she recalls Muslim students in her school district wearing yellow stickers with the star and crescent symbol representing Islam,[28] an allusion to the yellow badges that have been used to mark Jews since the Middle Ages,[29] most notably during the Holocaust.[30] The use of this kind of Holocaust imagery in anti-Islamophobia protests has been a source of contention, with individuals saying that drawing connections across history in a way that lacks sensitivity and understanding and only serves to provoke and offend.[31]

Elisheva, an Ohio-based Jewish Instagrammer whom we'll meet in more depth later, remembers receiving "compliments" in which people told her she looked like Anne Frank. While her Judaism was never exactly a secret, most of her peers didn't know about that facet of her identity until she mentioned it during a high school lesson on immigration in an English class. "It wasn't something I was particularly proud of; it was just a fact. But it led to a series of jokes. People told me I looked like Anne Frank, and that I looked like a f—ing Jew. I cried to my mom, but she told me not to take it personally." Elisheva's harassment continued, with swastikas appearing on her notebooks. When she reported this to the administration of her school, she was told they couldn't do anything about it. At that point, her Judaism went from a simple fact to a source of shame. She internalized a new message: "Being Jewish isn't something I should advertise." Like Jews from times and places throughout history, Elisheva lapsed into a state of hiddenness. While she did not actively deny who she was, by keeping her Judaism under wraps and separate from her public-facing identity, Elisheva did not live as her authentic self.

Living with the reality of the Holocaust and the collective memory of this atrocity has colored my experiences as a Jewish educator and broadly as an individual. When statistics like the 2020 Pew Report on the American Jewish community show how all-encompassing the Holocaust is when it comes to its role in identity, they cannot go unnoticed. In 2020's landmark study, 76 percent of American Jews said that remembering the Holocaust is essential to being Jewish.[32] The converse of this is that only 15 percent of Jews said that observing Jewish law is essential to their experiences of being Jewish. Knowing this, it brings up the question of how Holocaust education should be prioritized moving forward. Does focusing on this as the seminal event of the experience of the Jewish people maintain a sense of victimhood? Or, as many of the educators profiled expressed, is the Holocaust a backdrop against which personal meaning making for the twenty-first century can ultimately be achieved? Brad, who works in the field of antisemitism education, "As we become more removed from the Holocaust, it becomes an abstraction and a memory. It's not as acute, and that's obviously going to have a changing impact on how we see ourselves and its place in our world."

My own Holocaust education came to a climax during my first trip to Poland. This part of the twenty-first century Jewish experience included pilgrimage stops in Warsaw and Krakow, at the yeshiva in Lublin and memorials in small towns, and of course, the death camps. Traipsing across the country, I numbly saw ovens in Auschwitz, a pile of ashes the size of a small hill in Majdanek, and the stark woods that surrounded Treblinka. My group sang songs of Jewish pride at a memorial in the trees where children had been shot at close range. I found myself with no tears, no words, just wide eyes, silently observing the remnants of communities and people who once laughed, loved, and lived. There is a sense of survivor's guilt, a concurrent relief at not having been subjected to this hell and embarrassment at being weak in the face of such suffering and strength. Bailey, the New York-based college student, described Jewish guilt as she'd conveyed it to a friend. "It's an obligation to continue a legacy. And also a fear. There's a history of people not wanting you."

I remember throwing up in an alleyway in a small town. We had just finished holding an impromptu prayer service near a stone that served as a marker for the mass grave for the Jews of the town who had been massacred. The stone stood in the courtyard that served as a backyard for three row houses off the main town square. Next to this black mark were children's toys and a play set, and in the cold night air, as my companions and I shivered through the words of the memorial prayer, I saw eyes on us from the houses. All of a sudden, just as when I was a child, the barrier between past and present didn't seem to exist. I realized that in rural Poland, there isn't much transience. So the people who were there at that moment, watching us, were likely the descendants of those who had been there then, watching, or, God forbid, participating, in the massacre. I was overwhelmed. I felt the cold but only through the layers I'd piled on, insulating myself with the privilege of the twenty-first century. I felt the eyes staring at me because I didn't belong there. Because we were ghosts. Ghosts of a past too painful to remember but too raw to forget.

NOTES

1. Philologos (2017, June 21). What is the source of the phrase "never again"? *Mosaic Magazine.*

2. Popescu, D. I., & Schult, T. (2019). Performative Holocaust commemoration in the 21st century. *Holocaust Studies, 26*(2), 135–136. Retrieved from https://doi.org/10.1080/17504902.2019.1578452

3. Buettner, A. (2016). Never again: Rwanda, genocide, and the Holocaust. In *Holocaust images and picturing catastrophe: The cultural politics of seeing* (p. 85). Abingdon, UK: Routledge.

4. How the Holocaust motto never again became a rallying cry for gun control (2018, March 8). Jewish Telegraphic Agency.

5. Burack, E. (2018). Never again: From a Holocaust phrase to a universal phrase. *Jerusalem Post.* Retrieved from https://www.jpost.com/diaspora/never-again-from-a-holocaust-phrase-to-a-universal-phrase-544666

6. Alper, B. A. (2015). 70 years after WWII, the Holocaust is still very important to American Jews. Pew Research Center. Retrieved from https://www.pewresearch.org/fact-tank/2015/08/13/70-years-after-wwii-the-holocaust-is-still-very-important-to-american-jews

7. Alper, B. A., & Cooperman, A. (2021, May 11). 10 key findings about Jewish Americans. Pew Research Center. Retrieved from https://www.pewresearch.org/fact-tank/2021/05/11/10-key-findings-about-jewish-americans

8. Anti-Defamation League (n.d.). Six gorillion. Retrieved from https://www.adl.org/education/references/hate-symbols/six-gorillion

9. The United States Holocaust Museum (n.d.). *Fundamentals of teaching the Holocaust: Age appropriateness.* Retrieved from https://www.ushmm.org/teach/fundamentals/age-appropriateness

10. The Economist (2020). A memorial and a name. Retrieved from https://www.economist.com/graphic-detail/2020/01/25/archivists-are-racing-to-identify-every-jewish-holocaust-victim

11. My Jewish Learning (n.d.). The Passover (Pesach) seder. Retrieved from https://www.myjewishlearning.com/article/the-passover-pesach-seder

12. Jewish Virtual Library (n.d.). Modern Jewish history: The Spanish expulsion (1492). Retrieved from https://www.jewishvirtuallibrary.org/the-spanish-expulsion-1492

13. Lind, D. (2017, August 12). Unite the right, the violent white supremacist rally in Charlottesville, explained. Vox.

14. Beorn, W. W. (2018, June 20). Yes, you can call the border centers "concentration camps," but apply the history with care. *Washington Post.*

15. Holmes, J. (2019, June 13). An expert on concentration camps says that's exactly what the US is running at the border. *Esquire.* Retrieved from https://www.esquire.com/news-politics/a27813648/concentration-camps-southern-border-migrant-detention-facilities-trump

16. Sales, B. (2019, July 8). These Jews called out AOC over her use of "concentration camps." Here's what they think about the detention centers. *Jewish Telegraphic Agency.* Retrieved from https://www.jta.org/2019/07/08/united-states/these-jews-called-out-aoc-over-her-use-of-concentration-camps-heres-what-they-think-about-the-detention-centers

17. Glaun, D. (2019, July 15). "Never again": Why Jewish protesters in Boston are comparing border detention facilities to concentration camps. MASS Live. Retrieved from https://www.masslive.com/news/2019/07/never-again-holocaust-comparisons-in-immigration-protests-expose-rift-among-jewish-groups.html

18. The United States Holocaust Memorial Museum (n.d.). Where Holocaust education is required in the US. *The United States Holocaust Memorial Museum.* Retrieved from https://www.ushmm.org/teach/fundamentals/where-holocaust-education-is-required-in-the-us

19. VOA News (2020, September 16). Survey finds lack of Holocaust knowledge among American young adults. Voice of America. Retrieved from https://www.voanews.com/usa/survey-finds-lack-holocaust-knowledge-among-american-young-adults

20. Rojas, N. (2018, December 13). Alter Weinter, 92-year-old who survived Auschwitz during the Holocaust, killed by car. *Newsweek*. Retrieved from https://www.newsweek.com/alter-wiener-92-year-old-survived-auschwitz-during-holocaust-killed-car-1257400

21. Alter, C. (2018, March 22). The school shooting generation has had enough. *Time*. Retrieved from https://time.com/longform/never-again-movement

22. Sudakow, J. (2017, August 16). A good story is always far more persuasive than facts and figures. *Inc*. Retrieved from https://www.inc.com/james-sudakow/why-a-good-story-is-far-more-persuasive-than-facts.html

23. Zauzmer, J. (2018, April 12). Holocaust study: Two-thirds of millennials don't know what Auschwitz is. *The Washington Post*. Retrieved from https://www.washingtonpost.com/news/acts-of-faith/wp/2018/04/12/two-thirds-of-millennials-dont-know-what-auschwitz-is-according-to-study-of-fading-holocaust-knowledge

24. Pew Research Center (2020, January 22). What Americans know about the Holocaust. Retrieved from https://www.pewforum.org/2020/01/22/what-americans-know-about-the-holocaust

25. Pew Research Center (2019, October 3). For a lot of American teens, religion is a regular part of the public school day. Retrieved from https://www.pewforum.org/2019/10/03/methodology-27

26. O'Brien, M. (2020, October 12). Facebook bans Holocaust denial, distortion posts. Associated Press. Retrieved from https://apnews.com/article/election-2020-media-social-media-elections-mark-zuckerberg-14e8073ce6f7bd2a674c99ac7bbfc240

27. Friedberg, E. (2018, December 12). Why Holocaust analogies are dangerous. United States Holocaust Memorial Museum. Retrieved from https://www.ushmm.org/information/press/press-releases/why-holocaust-analogies-are-dangerous

28. Glassé, C. (2001). "Moon." *The new encyclopedia of Islam* (revised edition). Rowman & Littlefield Publishers, New York, p. 314.

29. Levy, R. S., Bell, D. P., Donahue, W. C., Madigan, K., Morse, J., Shevitz, A. H., & Stillman, N. A. (2005). *Antisemitism: A historical encyclopedia of prejudice and persecution*. Santa Barbara, CA: ABC-CLIO, volume 1, p. 779.

30. United States Holocaust Memorial Museum (n.d.). Jewish badge: During the Nazi era. Retrieved from https://encyclopedia.ushmm.org /content/en/article/jewish-badge-during-the-nazi-era

31. Chen, M. (2015, December 21). Badges aimed at Islamophobia spark controversy. ABC News San Diego. Retrieved from https://www.10news .com/news/badge-using-nazi-era-yellow-stars-sparks-criticism-122115

32. Sales, B. (2021, May 11). 10 key takeaways from the new Pew survey of American Jews. *Times of Israel*. Retrieved from https://www .timesofisrael.com/10-key-takeaways-from-the-new-pew-survey-of -american-jews

THREE

#Jewish: Telling Their Stories via Social Media

The power of social media is that it forces necessary change.

—Erik Qualman

"Gen Z knows you can make a difference through your fingertips, and they have the tools to do it." Hannah is a passionate young Jewish leader. During the COVID-19 pandemic, she decided to use Instagram and Tik-Tok to make a personal project public. Hannah is the granddaughter of a Holocaust survivor, and when the pandemic forced people indoors and behind screens, she chose to use hers to document her grandfather's story. With posts exploring his life before, during, and after the Holocaust, Hannah created an engaging account and used the platforms of her social media accounts to educate others on the legacy of the Holocaust. In doing so, she stepped into an immersive world to literally meet her target audience in one of their most visited locations. "Generation Z is used to hyper-stimulation, so when you're communicating with them, you have to understand them." Theirs is a world that has infinite possibilities, all accessible at the touch of a finger. For some, it can feel impenetrable, with trends changing instantaneously and platforms updating and evolving just as you get the hang of the existing model. For others, it's practically inescapable. After all, social media apps are designed to keep users scrolling and streaming, spending more and more of their time in the pose that has come to define connecting in the twenty-first century: head tilted down toward the smartphone, a single finger moving, ready to like, swipe, and engage. As of June 2020, 62 percent of parents with a teenager between the ages of fourteen and seventeen at home said that their teens spent upwards of four hours a day on their personal electronic devices since the start of the COVID-19 pandemic. Prior to the pandemic and within that same demographic, only 32 percent of parents reported that level of usage.[1] It is understood that social media and adolescence are ubiquitous at this point.

Social media is often a double-edged sword. It has clear benefits for teens, particularly those who are seeking a community that they are not able to find in other areas of their lives. According to the Mayo Clinic, the networks that social media provides can offer teens valuable support, particularly those who experience exclusion or who have disabilities or chronic illnesses.[2] It can be used for both entertainment and self-expression, and it is used by teens to expose themselves to current events, debates, and trends. Hannah referenced the use of social media with regard to her confidence in the power of Generation Z. "What gives me hope about this generation is how engaged and informed they are about what's going on in the world. . . . There's so much of an opportunity to reach them." However, despite the access, information, and escape that it affords, extensive social media usage is understood to be correlated with heightened risk for mental health issues.[3]

It's easy for social media to be written off by older generations. It's a time sucker. We can wax nostalgic for what it was like to grow up without the quest for "likes" driving our actions and bemoan that Generation Zers are more likely to express their appreciation for their friends by double-tapping a photo than by picking up the phone and calling them. We can roll our eyes at experiences and food being judged based on how Instagrammable they are and at viral challenges that sometimes veer into the dangerous.[4] None of that is inaccurate, and all of it is understandable. But what is wrong is writing off these platforms, their impact, and the Generation Zers who have learned how to harness it all.

Hannah shared some of the positive experiences she's seen come out of social media activism. She connected with a non-Jewish high school sophomore from Kentucky who came across her Holocaust-related TikTok videos. His interest in the Holocaust had been piqued when he saw videos of his peers visiting Auschwitz and other death camps and making light of their experiences at these sites. He was disheartened to see this kind of disrespect and turned to the power of the internet to build community engagement as his answer. He began a petition calling on the Polish government to establish an honor/sentinel guard at Auschwitz. In his own words on his Change.org petition, "People will know that what happened here has not been forgotten and that these people's memories are still alive. I started this petition to get closure and respect for the families and those who saved lives in Auschwitz. My project's goal is to preserve the history that many people have forgotten."[5] As of this writing, over 3,700 people signed his petition. Whether or not the call to action leads to a change at Auschwitz, the use of social media as a rallying point is telling of both its real and perceived power to alter the status quo.

Social media has created a reality wherein Generation Zers have unprecedented access to organizations and influencers who would have been out of reach in previous generations. It has also created an ever-growing cadre of individuals who have chosen to use the platforms available to them to become influencers themselves. By creating social media presences that are followed and even respected, Generation Zers are able to curate and produce content that shares their perspectives and worldviews and gives glimpses into their inner selves to their followers. Jewish social media influencers often showcase their practices and beliefs, and they educate others accordingly.

Ella, Jenny, and Amy are three Jewish high school students from California, Massachusetts, and Illinois, respectively. The three girls met through their participation in an Israel advocacy fellowship through an international Israel education organization. They come from varying Jewish backgrounds and paths to involvement. Ella, a high school senior in Los Angeles, goes to a Christian-affiliated high school. She heard her peers calling Judaism "watered-down Christianity." While she said she never felt that antisemitism, or even antisemitic microaggressions, had a major impact on her, when she began the process of applying to college and writing her essays, she reflected and realized that an undercurrent was always there.

Jenny is from the Boston suburbs and attended a public high school. She didn't grow up in an area with a large Jewish community but started to connect with her Judaism through her youth group. As she became more involved, she started to notice the multiple manifestations of antisemitism in her life and realized that she didn't have to be alone in this knowledge. Through their fellowship, the three girls began a project: an Instagram account. Its stated goal is to provide a space for middle school and high school students to submit stories of antisemitism that happen in their respective schools. These stories are then shared on the Instagram account, which regularly tags the schools themselves in the posts, creating not only a community of awareness and support but also of accountability.

In the past, Jenny has felt the isolation that can come from being singled out on social media, particularly as a Jewish person. "I was once called out because I posted something about how all these people are posting in solidarity with Black Lives Matter, but no one ever talks about the rise in antisemitism. And immediately someone, someone who I thought was my friend, said that because I don't post *enough* about Black Lives Matter and antiracism, I don't have the right to comment." In the past few years, social media activism has taken off, particularly on Instagram, with users sharing information in the form of infographics relating to the issues that matter to them. The goal is raising awareness and drawing attention to the cause being highlighted. However, the sharing of these infographics has become known as performative activism, with the individuals who share the graphics rarely participating in direct action such as attending related protests, donating to nonprofit organizations, or volunteering.[6] For Generation Z, though, what's seen by peers and followers is critical to the image of activism and allyship, and Jenny's perceived silence on a key topic opened her to judgment and dissent.

Their Instagram account aims to do just the opposite. According to Amy, "this account is to give students the support they need. It's essential for these students to be able to talk about the issue without feeling pressured or unsafe. The fact that we provide that space is pretty awesome." When the account became active, the stories began coming, demonstrating to followers that when it comes to antisemitism in schools, little is off limits. There are stories of peers, stories of teachers, stories of school policies coming in from schools around the world.

A few of the anonymous confessions:

"In seventh grade I experienced antisemitism for the first time. We covered the Holocaust and it was hard for me in class. The two guys sitting next to me thought it would be funny to follow me around and do the Heil Hitler thing. It was awful. They would follow me around and also drew a swastika on my desk in Sharpie."

"My sophomore year, I was sent a lot of antisemitic memes in a group chat for a school club. I was told to get into a gas chamber, faced Hitler memes, and then was told that I was 'overreacting' when I was upset. I took screenshots and told them to the sponsor of the club, who was a teacher. He ignored it. The main person who sent the antisemitic memes was given an award for being a kind person by that same teacher."

"In my painting class, we had an assignment to paint a famous figure throughout history. A student chose to paint Hitler. The portrait was completely glorifying him and he was dressed in swastikas and every-thing. It was hung up in the classroom as the student was working on it, and many students felt incredibly uncomfortable. As a Jewish student, I especially felt uncomfortable and went to the counselors office about it. Nothing happened. The portrait stayed, and the student faced no consequences."

"One day in my AP World [History] class we were discussing the oppression of minorities. It was a group assignment where we would dis-cuss things during class. Every time I tried to speak about the oppression of Jews I would be immediately shut down because 'Jews are white so they can't be oppressed.' Another time a girl told me that Jews own every-thing and are always rich, so we were never oppressed. After that day, I was just shocked. My perspective of my school changed, and I just didn't feel safe."

Each of these confessions is a snapshot in time. They demonstrate trends in twenty-first-century antisemitism that are both enlightening and disturb-ing: the continued preponderance of Holocaust imagery when it comes to isolating and attacking Jews; the reluctance of others, whether peers or authority figures, to step in as allies. And somehow, all of the recipients of this treatment have turned to social media and an anonymous Instagram account as their outlet. There are no guarantees that sharing their stories will have any impact. All the moderators of the account can offer is a "shout-out" to their schools via Instagram. It may not help. It may make things worse. But it's the forum that they have to express themselves, to read and know that they aren't alone, and to be validated in the knowledge that their experiences are legitimate, are upsetting, and are worthy of allyship.

Social media, in addition to providing outlets for Generation Zers to find fellowship and camaraderie in the face of hate in their "real lives" also gives emerging activists and educators a platform from which they are capable of reaching and impacting lives around the world. Elisheva is one of these emerging voices for the Jewish community online. She is the cre-ator of an Instagram account that exists at the intersection of her two iden-tities: Jewish and Romani. Elisheva identifies as a member of both the Jewish community and the Roma people, a European ethnic minority often pejoratively referred to as Gypsies. Elisheva, like many of her peers, comes from an interfaith family. In 2013, it was reported that 44 percent of Jews who married chose a non-Jewish partner, including 58 percent of those who had married since 2005, both numbers that have only increased since that time.[7] In Elisheva's case, her mother identifies as Jewish while her father is Romani, creating Elisheva's intersectional lived experience within the wider context of the Jewish community. "I had no idea anyone else like me existed. But now, I've made this whole community on the internet. People reach out to me all the time to say thank you or to tell me how much they've learned from me."

Elisheva started her Instagram account at the encouragement of her friends and has had positive experiences on the platform as well as on Tik-Tok, where she posts funny, self-deprecating videos about her dual identities. But she has also seen the dark side of what expressing herself on social media opens her up to when it comes to detractors and hate speech. She has received numerous messages from neo-Nazis, telling her that they wish Hitler had killed *both* sides of her family. She has also received comments on videos about seemingly innocent topics such as taste testing gefilte fish, a traditional Ashkenazi Jewish food. "I posted my gefilte fish video on TikTok and immediately people started responding with Free Palestine. Most of them were anonymous, and I think they feel like there aren't any consequences for them that way."

Sophie is a high school senior from Chicago who recently moved with her family to the Southwest. She has always identified as Jewish and began to truly connect with this aspect of herself through the lens of social justice. She began an accompanying Instagram account "to rant about what was going on, and how alone I felt regarding antisemitism. And people started listening to me." Sophie's account focuses on the intersection of Judaism and social justice and became what she describes as a "safe space" for her self-expression on social media, as well as a place to educate others. "When I expressed my Judaism on my personal account, I would get threats, so I created a space where I could just put it all out there."

In Sophie's experience, Jews tend to keep quiet as a response to antisemitism instead of speaking out. "I tend to minimize online antisemitism because it feels like it's online and not 'real life.'" Despite Sophie's self-described nonconfrontational style, she has been inspired to be both an advocate within the Jewish community and an ally outside of it. "After seeing truly pervasive antisemitism in the Trump era, I've evolved in the face of that. It's made me want to fight for others as well."

Another Jewish activist and ally, Arielle, a high school senior from Connecticut, has an Instagram bio that sums up the complexities of her Jewish identity:

- She/her
- Religious Ashkenazi
- Your friendly neighborhood Jew
- Here to empower the voices of Jewish and BIPOC[8] communities

She began her educational Instagram presence with the goal of providing insights into the complexities of Judaism and Jewish identity for a broad audience. Believing that much of hate is actually ignorance, she felt that by educating a wide, non-Jewish audience about the intricacies of Judaism could be her contribution to countering antisemitism and spreading awareness. In pursuit of that goal of education, Arielle provided posts about different kinds of Jews—Ashkenazi, Sephardic, Karaite, Jews of Color—as well as Jewish practices and beliefs. She lived the dichotomy of the pluses and minuses of being visibly Jewish on social media. She found a community online, becoming part of a cadre of Jewish content creators. As one of the only Jews in her high school, she's been thrilled to find like-minded peers online. At the same time, she's had enough experiences to be able to delineate: TikTok is more antisemitic than Instagram. Posts about Jewish holidays may be "flag-bombed," but Israel- or Zionism-focused posts generate much more hatred. TikTok is where she's experienced people telling her to go to the ovens. But after posting about her experiences with antisemitism, she received an outpouring of support.

"Social media isn't a waste of time when you're engaging with other members of your community, and it's a tool for activism and connecting with others. Don't underestimate it." Arielle, like many other Jewish social media content creators, is using her own voice to amplify the voices of others. She uses her platform as an ally, highlighting how Jewish values connect with activism, the Black Lives Matter movement, and social justice as a part of the Jewish experience. Arielle's online activism is inspired by her understanding of the intersectional nature of hate. She, like many Generation Zers,[9] holds that the problems that progressive activists face are all linked by white supremacy. "Antisemitism, racism, sexism . . . they're all part of a system, and by engaging across those lines, we can be more effective in our collective activism."

Social media activism and education have been points of contention for Jewish communal professionals and commentators since their inception. In 2019, the Eva Stories project was launched on Instagram. This interactive media piece turned the real-life Holocaust-era diary of Eva Heyman into a series of Instagram (and, subsequently, SnapChat) stories that appeared over the course of several days, sharing Eva's experiences before and during World War II as a series of videos and interactive experiences on Instagram. Ultimately, Eva died at the age of thirteen in Auschwitz-Birkenau, and her diary was subsequently found and published by Yad Vashem, Israel's Holocaust memorial museum.[10] But compared to the *Diary of Anne Frank*, which in many ways has become synonymous with Holocaust adolescent literature and is often the first exposure that students will have via middle school and high school reading lists, Eva's words remained relatively unknown before content creators Mati and Maya Kochavi, a father-daughter team, made the decision to put Eva on Instagram.

Of the experience, Mati said, "If we want to bring the memory of the Holocaust to the young generation, we have to bring it to where they are . . . and they're on Instagram."[11] The Eva.Stories account quickly generated over one million followers, and the high production quality of the videos, as well as their accessibility, was simultaneously praised and criticized.[12] While Eva.Stories falls on one end of the spectrum when it comes to the Holocaust on social media, as a thoughtful, researched, and respectful experiential piece, and offensive misinformation is the obvious other, the gray area that falls in between is often the space where many Generation Zers struggle to define antisemitism online. One of the most cited examples is that of the "Holocaust selfie" phenomenon. Many visitors to Holocaust memorials across Europe take selfies to post on their social media accounts. According to an analysis, the majority of photos taken at Holocaust sites are respectful, being tagged with hashtags such as #tragic, #remembrance, and #sadness.[13] But other photos seem more inherently disrespectful, with individuals doing everything from "taking photos posing next to razor wire, selfies with victim's hair in the background, and even group shots in front of the crematoria."[14] When social media is the vehicle through which one is accustomed to telling stories, and the tough content of Judaism, the Holocaust, and antisemitism is the content one strives to get across, the question of where the line between sensitive and offensive lies is blurred and still developing.

Using social media, and particularly interactive video game platforms, can often be the first exposure that young Generation Zers have not only to outright antisemitism but also to questions about their Judaism. Abbi recalls that when her son was in the fourth grade, he and his friends were playing Fortnite, a multiplayer online game. Her son mentioned being Jewish, which the other kids began to question. "What does that mean?

Do you believe in God?" As Abbi recounts the story, her son replied that yes, he believes in God, but not in Jesus as the son of God. Another player told him that was wrong, but he was able to reply, "You might think that's wrong, but that's what I believe, and I believe what I believe. You can believe what you believe." While the innocent questions of a fellow fourth grader do not pass the barometer of antisemitism, being in a position of needing to speak for Judaism and the Jewish people from a young age is the first step in what will likely be a lifelong journey. Abbi notes, "The video game conversation was the first time his religion has come up as something that makes him different from his friends."

Hannah noted that "antisemitism on TikTok is almost a unifying experience because it's so universal. Everyone is experiencing it." Mara, the Binghamton University student, agreed. "On TikTok, sometimes even if you don't say anything explicitly Jewish, but you show certain social cues of being a Jewish teenage girl, and you're doing TikTok dances that are totally unrelated to Judaism and people can tell who you are, they'll comment 'Free Palestine.'" She continued in her reflection on the so-called flag bombing that she and so many of her Jewish peers have experienced on TikTok in particular. "Is it antisemitism when someone points out your Jewishness in an unhelpful way? Or is it just inappropriate? Like, if I'm doing a dance and not mentioning that I'm Jewish but you know and make it all about that, does it count? Or is it just awkward?"

Other instances Mara has experienced have been more clear-cut. "When people on Twitter say Anne Frank is a colonizer, that's antisemitism. It's also just dumb." In May 2021, during a one-week span of time, over seventeen thousand users posted iterations of the phrase "Hitler was right" on Twitter.[15] The ubiquity of Holocaust-based antisemitic rhetoric on social media demonstrates how easy it is for the internet to become a breeding ground for the spreading of misinformation (at best), hate, and ultimately, incitement to violence. According to Lisa, who works at an organization with the stated mission of using lessons of history to challenge teachers and their students to stand up to bigotry and hate,[16] social media like this is leading to a rise in Holocaust denial. "We're not just dealing with the loss of survivors but the media and what media students are following. It impacts how they see the truth. And over the last number of years, there's been a degradation of fact." Brad, whose professional portfolio focuses on fighting antisemitism on a nationwide scale, agreed. "This generation is getting a steady, daily dose of antisemitic images via social media."

Brad cautions those monitoring such issues to not take the antisemitism and Holocaust denial happening on social media lightly. He describes a dichotomy experienced by the Jewish community, wherein there is either a perception that "it's not a real threat and we don't have to worry . . . or it's the Holocaust [in terms of extremity]." He emphasizes the need to take a more nuanced approach, because things like the Holocaust don't just happen overnight. "It takes conditioning. It's the jokes told in German beer halls, it's the slurs that dehumanize people, it's the microaggressions and the off-color remarks, and slowly, slowly, it's not wanting to play with the Jewish kids, not letting them play on your basketball teams, and it builds."

During the 2020 COVID-19 pandemic, the line between virtual life and in-person life blurred in unprecedented ways. As gathering spaces, social interactions, and life cycle events transitioned to virtual platforms, these ways of connecting took an even greater precedence in the lives of Generation Zers. Out of all demographic groups, Generation Z demonstrated the largest increase in media consumption during the period of the COVID-19 outbreak.[17] During the pandemic, it was found that the average Generation Zer interacted on at least five digital platforms daily. They are aware of the complexities of how these platforms, and the people who post on them, operate. More than half of Generation Zers, as well as millennials, reported being "very aware" of "fake news" surrounding the pandemic and were able to spot inaccurate posts. However, they were not particularly likely to counter such posts, with over 35 percent of Generation Zers ignoring and scrolling past false posts.[18] This propensity to be able to recognize false postings on social media but to not necessarily engage with them is replicated when it comes to Jewish (and anti-Jewish) content on these same platforms.

"Every time I see something antisemitic or something false about Israel on social media, I feel like I have to make a choice. Am I going to comment back and get into a whole spam war over it? Or should I just let it go and keep scrolling and not engage?" When Elana shared this dilemma, which she faces every time a friend, an influencer, or an organization that she follows or looks up to disappoints her by implicitly or explicitly espousing antisemitism, it emphasized how personally and with how much thought she and her peers approach their social media relationships. There is a sense of responsibility and mutualism in the way that Generation Zers approach the social media spaces they spend time in. "I know that if I say something, I'll probably get dragged into a whole thing and people will come at me. But if I don't, then everyone else who sees whatever the post is has to deal with the same thing, and they don't know that there are people there who are on their side."

Elana's sense of responsibility to the largely anonymous individuals to whom she is only connected in the sense that they follow the same people demonstrates the importance that online communities have to Generation Zers. Nearly three-quarters of Generation Zers and millennials surveyed said that belonging to an online community improved their sense of unity in the world, and 77 percent said that it has improved their overall well-being. Sixty percent of Generation Z in particular said that online community support is very important to them, and they are the most likely generation to feel that their online community better understands their passions than their family and friends do.[19] With this understanding of how critical online communities, and the influencers who create and curate them, are to Generation Z, it demonstrates how damaging it can be to see otherwise trusted individuals readily and freely share antisemitic content online.

During the May 2021 outbreak of violence between Israelis and Palestinians,[20] 60 percent of Jewish Americans reported personally witnessing antisemitism as a result of the conflict. When it came to online antisemitism in particular, 75 percent of American Jews considered the statement that Israel should not exist as a Jewish state to be an antisemitic sentiment. Comparing Israel's actions to those of the Nazis was seen as antisemitic by 70 percent; calling Zionism racist (61 percent) and calling Israel an apartheid state (55 percent) were considered by the majority of Jews to be definitely or probably antisemitic.[21] While Generation Zers are not alone in encountering the ubiquitous antisemitism of the internet, in many instances it is falling to young people to be the voices countering the misinformation that is otherwise rampant on social media.

When it comes to the value of such interactions, journalist Ben Sales posed these questions: Does that fight [over Israel and Judaism] create space for substantive dialogue or narrow it? Can a crusade to combat antisemitism distort our understanding of it? What does it do to the mental and emotional health of those involved? Is social media, with algorithms that incentivize division and anger, and policies that have long been criticized for tolerating hate speech, the right arena for this debate?[22]

The question of whether or not the social media wars, the latest iteration of the war for hearts and minds, are valuable, is of course an important one. But for Generation Z, coming of age with their online worlds holding the same importance as their in-person realities, it almost misses the point. The fights engaged in on social media are unproductive at best and are all too often emotionally draining or frightening. But sometimes, for Jewish Americans coming to terms with what it means to be proud of their identities, expressing themselves and standing up for themselves on social media is an expression of their Judaism.

In the 2020 report on Jewish Americans, it was found that 4 percent of Jewish adults participate in online conversations about Judaism and being Jewish.[23] While this number does not delineate how responding to antisemitism factors into that percentage—and indeed if seeing or reacting to antisemitism is encompassed in how respondents thought of what it means to participate in conversations about Judaism—it can be seen as demonstrative of what it means for Generation Zers to "own" their Judaism online. It cannot be assumed that for a Generation Zer, to actively engage with Judaism online is a given. Like the vast majority of Jewish adults in their lives, it would be easy for Generation Zers not to showcase their Jewish identities and instead to focus on the other facets of their intersectional selves as their online personas. Indeed, a quick scroll through Instagram or Twitter shows how easy it is to build a robust online presence without any substance whatsoever, or with platitudes and memes shared about the cause du jour, without necessarily having a personal connection to any of it. For aspiring influencers, that may be the smarter move: portraying a whitewashed version of themselves that doesn't open them up to controversy and vitriol.

By understanding how easy it is for over 95 percent of Jews to opt out of regularly engaging Jewishly online, we can then develop an appreciation for those Generation Zers who are actively bucking that trend and doing the opposite. It makes sense that if social media is an extension of one's social life, it will include many, if not all, of the facets of "real life." With both the positives and the negatives on full display at times, Jewish Generation Zers are figuring out how to make responsible social media choices that are authentic to their whole selves. Part of this, as an unfortunate reality, calls for them making choices, often on a moment's notice, about antisemitism. Ella, the Los Angeles–based high school student, noted that she often tries to give people she follows the benefit of the doubt. "A lot of people don't hate Jewish people, but they have a lot of resentment based on misinformation and antisemitism that no one ever told them is wrong." Rather than automatically assuming the worst, Ella uses her platform and knowledge to educate and to counter the spread of falsehoods. At the same time, she has seen that in many cases, "antisemitism is more covert and hidden." For adolescents still figuring out the intricacies of their own Jewish journey, identifying the antisemitic tropes and falsehoods regularly shared online is a challenge that calls for support and empowerment rather than critique.

For Jewish parents and educators alike, there is a desire to protect the adolescents in their care from the hate that may be directed toward them. Nicki, a North Carolina–based mother, shared her dilemmas. "Do we send our son out of our zoned school district so he can be in a space where Hebrew classes are offered and there are other Jewish kids? Or do we keep him in our zone, where he'd be one of very few? We don't want him to be in a bubble where the first time he experiences difference is when he goes away to college. . . . We want to have the ability to have difficult conversations." Finding the balance between providing opportunities for difficult and complex topics while creating a safe space for self-expression and identification is a challenge made even greater when hate can buzz into someone's hand at literally any moment.

Nicki continued, "I hope that even if my kids don't face antisemitism directly, that they're aware of what's out there, and they know how they can respond. I want them to be ready to stand up." Social media, for many, may be the first place that they feel called upon to stand up and speak out as young Jews. Knowing this, and particularly knowing how early this exposure may take place as smartphones enter the picture at increasingly younger ages,[24] there is a drive to educate early and often.

Mara, the SUNY student, noted that, particularly in the context of Israel education, despite years of camp, involvement in a youth movement, and attendance at a Jewish day school, too much of her education came too late. "Especially when you're younger, your education makes you more of a fan of Israel—its music, food, tourism, whatever—than a believer in the right of the Jewish people to self-determination. There's such a great opportunity in Jewish education, and it goes to waste. We need a more academic understanding of the ideas behind Judaism and Zionism. It can't just be saying the Torah says this and leaving it there. It has to be more than that. Self-determination is not a concept that had been explained to me until I was fifteen, and for a lot of people, by then it's too late. All I felt like I really knew about was food."

While very few would think of social media as a platform of the sharing of meaningful and complex content, this call for a more robust education about Judaism and Israel that can be used to respond to detractors and questioners demonstrates how seriously Generation Zers take their roles. They are craving more—more knowledge, more content, more connection that takes into account their ability to engage with complexities—that will surely only enhance their respective capabilities to proactively share their emerging Jewish stories and to react appropriately to the hate that unfortunately continues to pervade many spaces.

Social media brings out the worst in people and also the best. Anyone who has spent time in certain forums is all too familiar with internet trolls: individuals who scour different sites, spewing vitriol and hate. But hopefully, they have also seen the beauty: the allies, coming out of the ether to defend those who are vulnerable in any given moment; the cheerleaders, championing one another through the best and the worst that life has to offer, often without knowing each other beyond the confines of a screen and a scrolling thumbprint; the moments of connection that come when people find a kindred spirit that they didn't know existed before.

Antisemitism is a constant, but the ways that it manifests for Generation Z are markedly different than they have been for previous generations. The hate and the anger that are the markers of antisemitism literally come to the fingertips of Generation Zers, wherever they are. Even in the spaces that should be the safest, such as home, school, and forums where Generation Zers express themselves and communicate with their friends, the lurking hatred is always present, either on the edges or front and center. In many ways, social media is an evolving reality. There are constantly new platforms, new opportunities, and new concerns. For Generation Z, communicating in these spaces is like speaking in one's native tongue. As the world continues to adapt to an interconnected reality, the opportunities for antisemitism to morph continue growing just as much. Generation Z is at the forefront of these challenges, and supporting Generation Z as it meets them head on is the role of the Jewish community as well as its allies. What that looks like, however, is ultimately up to Generation Z.

NOTES

1. Johnson, J. (2021, January 27). U.S. kids & teens with 4hrs+ screen time before and during COVID-19 pandemic 2020. Statista. Retrieved from https://www.statista.com/statistics/1189204/us-teens-children-screen -time-daily-coronavirus-before-during

2. Mayo Clinic Staff. (2019, December 21). Teens and social media use: What's the impact? Retrieved from https://www.mayoclinic.org/healthy

-lifestyle/tween-and-teen-health/in-depth/teens-and-social-media-use
/art-20474437

3. Riehm, K. E., et al. (2019). Associations between time spent using social media and internalizing and externalizing problems among US youth. *JAMA Psychiatry*. Retrieved from https://doi.org/10.1001/jamapsychiatry.2019.2325

4. Bever, L. (2018, January 17). Teens are daring each other to eat Tide pods. We don't need to tell you that's a bad idea. *Washington Post*. Retrieved from https://www.washingtonpost.com/news/to-your-health/wp/2018/01/13/teens-are-daring-each-other-to-eat-tide-pods-we-dont-need-to-tell-you-thats-a-bad-idea

5. Barbour, C. (2020). Polish government: To establish an honor/sentinel guard at Auschwitz concentration camp. Change.org. Retrieved from https://www.change.org/p/polish-government-to-establish-an-honor-sentinel-guard-at-auschwitz-concentration-camp

6. Freedman, R. (2021, February 23). Performative social media activism is largely unproductive. *Berkeley High Jacket*. Retrieved from https://berkeleyhighjacket.com/2021/entertainment/performative-social-media-activism-is-largely-unproductive

7. Case, E. C. (2014). What we know about intermarried families. *Journal of Jewish Communal Service, 89*(1).

8. Black, Indigenous, People of Color.

9. Rutherford, J. (2020, July 20). Generation Z trends in the workplace: What employers need to know. Torch Light Hire. Retrieved from https://torchlighthire.com/generation-z-trends-in-the-workplace-what-employers-need-to-know

10. Holliday, L. (1995). *Children in the Holocaust and World War II*. Simon & Schuster, p. 99.

11. Holmes, O. (2019, May 8). Instagram Holocaust diary Eva. Stories sparks debate in Israel. *The Guardian*. Retrieved from https://www.theguardian.com/world/2019/may/08/instagram-holocaust-diary-evastories-sparks-debate-in-israel

12. Kershner, I. (2019, April 30). A Holocaust story for the social media generation. *New York Times*.

13. Commane, G., & Potton, R. (2019). Instagram and Auschwitz: A critical assessment of the impact social media has on Holocaust representation. *Holocaust Studies, 25*(1–2), 158–181.

14. Wight, C. A. (2020). Visitor perceptions of European Holocaust heritage: A social media analysis. *Tourism Management, 81*.

15. Mandel, B. (2021, May 24). 17,000 tweet "Hitler was right," and big tech barely reacts. *New York Post*. Retrieved from https://nypost.com /2021/05/24/17000-tweet-hitler-was-right-and-big-tech-barely-reacts

16. Facing History & Ourselves (n.d.). About us. Retrieved from https:// www.facinghistory.org/about-us

17. Clapp, R. (n.d.). Gen Z is driving changes in COVID-19 media habits. WARC. Retrieved from https://www.warc.com/content/paywall/article /gen-z-is-driving-changes-in-covid-19-media-habits/132150

18. World Health Organization (2021, March 26). Social media & COVID-19: A global study of digital crisis interaction among Gen Z and Millennials. Retrieved from https://www.who.int/news-room/feature-stories/detail/social -media-covid-19-a-global-study-of-digital-crisis-interaction-among-gen-z -and-millennials

19. Tapatalk (2019, July 25). Gen Z and Millennials feel more understood by specialized online communities compared to Facebook and IRL. PR Newswire. Retrieved from https://www.prnewswire.com/news-releases /gen-z-and-millennials-feel-more-understood-by-specialized-online-com munities-compared-to-facebook-and-irl-300890861.html

20.   https://www.youtube.com/watch?v=UOnSA5lxB1Q&feature= youtu.be

21. Anti-Defamation League (2021, June 9). Survey of American Jews since recent violence in Israel. Retrieved from https://www.adl.org/blog /survey-of-american-jews-since-recent-violence-in-israel

22. Sales, B. (2021, June 10). Young Zionist Jews say they're fighting antisemitism on social media. What are they accomplishing? Jewish Telegraphic Agency. Retrieved from https://www.jta.org/2021/06/10/united-states/young -zionist-jews-say-theyre-fighting-antisemitism-on-social-media-what-are -they-accomplishing

23. Pew Research Center (2021, May 11). Jewish Americans in 2020. Retrieved from https://www.pewforum.org/2021/05/11/jewish-americans -in-2020

24. Kamenetz, A. (2019, October 29). Report: More than half of U.S. children now own a smartphone by age 11. NPR. Retrieved from https:// www.npr.org/2019/10/29/774306250/report-more-than-half-of-u-s-children -now-own-a-smartphone-by-age-11

FOUR

Pittsburgh: The Day Safety Ended

On October 27, 2018, I was in Zbąszyń, Poland, as part of a trip with my extended family to commemorate the eightieth anniversary of the *Polenaktion* [Polish Action]; the deportation of 17,000 Jews with Polish citizenship who had been living in Germany. In October 1938, this first mass deportation of Jews from Germany under the Nazi regime involved the rounding up of men, women, and children, who were forcibly transported on trains across the border into Poland. Among these 17,000 individuals were my great-grandfather's brother, Leo Adler, and his son, Norbert. Norbert eventually survived the war. Leo was forced to dig his own grave on Rosh Hashanah, the Jewish new year. Together with 150 others, he was unceremoniously shot into it by Nazi machine gun fire.

Together with dozens of other Adler descendants, including Leo's last surviving child, his namesake grandson, and a new baby less than a year old, we journeyed to Berlin and Zbąszyń to walk the steps that Leo took when he was stolen from his family and rounded up with his fellow Jews. We visited the graves of ancestors who died before the war, proud and prominent members of German society. We laid a *Stolperstein*, literally a stumbling stone, a concrete cube with a brass plaque with the name and life dates of victims of Nazi extermination. Leo Adler's stone is now embedded in the cobblestones of a street in Berlin, outside what was once a loving family home. It gives the perfunctory details. He was born in 1898, was taken in the *Polenaktion*, and a year later, on September 16, 1939, was murdered by an *Einsatzgruppen* killing squad.

On October 27, it was a gray day in Poland. Together with cousins and representatives from other families whose ancestors had also been part of the *Polenaktion*, we woke up early, drove from Berlin across the border, and tramped through a now-sleepy town that once saw the worst of humanity's capacity to commit horrible acts against one another. We passed the same houses that had lined the streets when the deported Polish Jews saw them, and were mutely stared at by small, pale faces looking through the windows. In our honor, local high school students performed a play that they put on every year, recounting some of the stories of the town's role during World War II. We watched as teens embodied both Jewish deportees and Polish civilians, taking care to emphasize that both populations were ultimately victims of the Nazi regime, a choice in keeping with Polish governmental policies.[1]

I was predictably numb by the time my phone rang and I saw a call from my husband. He broke the news without preamble: there were reports of a shooting at a synagogue in Pittsburgh. I remember not fully processing the news. I'm an alumna of the University of Pittsburgh and count the Jewish community of Squirrel Hill as one of my own. I have two aunts who live within blocks of the Tree of Life–Or L'Simcha Congregation. They were with me in Zbąszyń that day, so while their safety was thankfully not a concern at that moment, the reality slowly began to sink in. It wouldn't fully process until the following day, when we saw the numbers and the names. Eighty years after the Polish Jews of Berlin were rounded up as the start of their ultimate destruction, the American Jewish community suffered its deadliest attack in history.

The Tree of Life massacre left eleven dead and six wounded. In addition to breaking the hearts of the families and friends of those who were murdered, as well as leaving a gaping wound in the Pittsburgh community, the shooting fundamentally shifted the sense of safety that the American Jewish community previously had. While as a New Yorker, and then a Washingtonian, my synagogues have had visible security presences for decades, almost immediately following the shooting, Jewish communities around the country began pouring funds into bulletproof glass, security vehicles, and defensive strategies. While these measures have been taken in order to increase a sense of safety and security for the Jewish community, Brad, whom we met earlier, noted, "It's not a positive thing that our communal spaces are fortresses and you have to step through armed security guards. It's great that the government is helping, but this is not exactly an ideal situation." For members of Generation Z, who hold the tragic distinction of being referred to as the mass-shooting generation,[2] the shooting brought home a hard-hit reality: not only are their schools not always safe places but neither are their houses of worship.

Rabbi Abbi S. is a Conservative rabbi. She works in the nonprofit sector, specializing in interfaith relationships. When the Tree of Life shooting happened, she found herself struggling with how to tell her then-young Generation Z son. Originally, she wasn't ready to share that news, that a synagogue had been targeted and, for some, could no longer be considered the safe space that it was in their family. However, her son was told about the events in Pittsburgh by a classmate and came home full of questions. "Why wasn't God stopping that person? Did the shooting happen because the people were Jewish?" In the months and years since the shooting, Abbi continues to wear a kippah, something that she says will not change. The family still has a mezuzah[3] on their front door, and lights an electric *chanukiah*[4] each Chanukah, which is prominently placed in their front window. But certain things have come into focus differently. "We will keep our voices down. Be respectful of others. We just are."

For Zachary, a high school student from the Washington, DC, area, whose grandmother is a congregant at Tree of Life–Or L'Simcha Congregation, the shooting was a call to action. While his grandmother was not in attendance at Shabbat services on the fateful day of October 27, 2018, the shooting hit close to home and spurred Zachary to action. He responded to his desire to create change by founding Generation Z Jews, an organization with the tagline "Fighting Anti-Semitism and Promoting Tikkun Olam."[5] In thinking about the days following the shooting, Zachary reflected, "Seeing something like [the shooting] so close to home made me realize that I don't want to grow up and live in a world where I have to be scared about being targeted just for being a Jew." This sense, that being a Jew in the United States means being a target for hate, is one that Generation Zers have had to come to terms with in new ways in the years since the shooting. College freshman Mara reflected, "I was deeply emotionally affected by the Tree of Life shooting. For me, the abstract idea of anti-semitism looms very large. I don't think about it on a day-to-day basis, but it's something I've been taught about. But that day was different."

Ezra, an Ohio-based high school freshman, was at the local Jewish Community Center with his mother when the news of the shooting came out. His mother found out first and broke the news, which hit perilously close to home. Like Zachary's grandmother, Ezra's grandfather is a congregant at Tree of Life. He was running late on the morning of October 27. So while Ezra's family was not marked by a personal loss in the shooting, they were part of the circle of communal mourning that impacted so many. Eli described his reaction to the shooting as shock, tears, and concern. The next day, on October 28, Ezra was invited to a friend's bat mitzvah celebration at a local Cleveland synagogue. For the first time, going to a synagogue felt different from the matter of course it had previously been. "I wasn't exactly scared. But I was on alert like I'd never been before. I was more aware, because now I knew what could happen." The next weekend, Ezra and his mother drove to the site of Tree of Life to see the memorial that sprung up, full of community tributes. Somber beyond his years, the day school alumnus, whose Jewish life is marked by ritual and community, noted his own transformation. "Before the shooting, I'd always heard about antisemitism. I knew about what *could* happen. But now it *did* happen, and it happened to my family, and it's deeper."

Dean, who works with high school students throughout the Midwest, placed the antisemitism of today into a historical context. "The American Jewish experience is unique because there was no emancipation. We're free, and equal, and discriminated against." The unique circumstances of the American Jewish experience hold that while there was never a time when Jews were denied citizenship, or full rights under the law, there is an underlying reality that antisemitism and discrimination have always been present in the American psyche. While this has most commonly manifested in what would be called microaggressions[6] in Generation Z–speak, in some incidents, like the massacre at Tree of Life–Or L'Simcha Congregation, the smoldering embers of antisemitism have reignited and burst into flames.

Melinda is a former employee of the Hebrew Immigrant Aid Society, which the Tree of Life shooter referenced only hours before committing the massacre. On the social network Gab, he wrote, "HIAS likes to bring invaders to kill our people. I can't sit by and watch my people get slaughtered. Screw your optics, I'm going in."[7] HIAS, founded in 1881, originally worked to aid Jews fleeing pogroms in the Russian Empire, subsequently expanding its reach to Jews from all over the world and, ultimately, growing to advocate for non-Jewish displaced people around the world. One of the congregations housed within the Tree of Life building, Dor Hadash, had participated in HIAS's annual National Refugee Shabbat the week before the shooting.[8]

As an employee of HIAS, and as the daughter of a survivor of a concentration camp, Melinda was impacted on multiple levels by the atrocity committed in Pittsburgh. Ultimately, she related to it as a mother. Only days after the shooting, Melinda went through the classic American rite of passage of taking her young daughter trick-or-treating for Halloween. This pastime was not one that Melinda herself had enjoyed as a child. Her parents were horrified by the idea of her "begging" from door to door in their neighborhood. But as a mother, Melinda found herself enjoying participating in the ritual and embracing the "transgressive spirit" of the holiday. However, on Halloween in 2018, still reeling from the shots fired and lives lost, the juxtaposition of frivolity and the weightiness of the world were at odds for Melinda. "Only a few days later, we were walking around the neighborhood dressed in symbols of death."

In the days following the shooting, connections were made between the attack and everything from *Kristallnacht*[9] to the pogroms.[10] These analogies demonstrate that for the American Jewish community, this watershed event was not an anomaly. Nor was it simply another example on the too-long list of mass shootings in the United States: 340 in total during 2018.[11] Instead, it was a link in a centuries-long chain of attacks on the Jewish people. For some, the shooting served as a wake-up call to the tenuousness of the feeling of safety that the American Jewish community had largely enjoyed. For others, it was a call to action, to advocacy, to speaking out. And to still others, it was a breaking point: the breaking of glass, the breaking of hearts, the shattering of lives.

For Bailey, the college student from North Carolina, the shooting at Tree of Life–Or L'Simcha Congregation was marked by the silence that followed. Bailey wasn't particularly involved in Jewish life at her college campus prior to the shooting. But in the aftermath of the shooting, she saw that in the progressive, academic circles that populated her college experience, there was a chilling quiet. "I saw the larger community not really react. The silence itself felt like a lack of caring about Jews, and I felt like I was the only one who cared about this major antisemitic event—I was the only one who was aware." This was the catalyst that led Bailey to seek out the Jewish community and find connections that felt authentic in the aftermath. "The shooting didn't change how I presented Jewishly. I was at school; it felt safe to engage with Judaism. But I felt a greater concern about how I presented and what it meant to be perceived as Jewish."

Alicia, a mother of a Generation Zer in Michigan, was worried about telling her preteen son about the shooting. "I expected him to be freaked out, and he wasn't. And I realized, I expected him to be scared because there was a shooting at a place he goes to every week [a synagogue]. But then I realized, he goes to school every day. Yes, we're targets in synagogues, but we're targets everywhere." Alicia recognized the reality of Generation Z, which has been marked by the proliferation of mass shootings in the United States, often in places where they're meant to feel safe, particularly schools. In a 2018 report, 75 percent of Generation Zers reported gun violence as a significant source of stress in their lives, with 72 percent specifically naming the possibility of school shootings as a stressor in their lives.[12] While efforts have been made to secure these spaces against gun violence, such as adding guards or metal detectors to entrances, more than one in five Generation Zers (22 percent) said that these measures actually *increased* their levels of stress related to school shootings, while 41 percent said that these efforts have done nothing for their stress either way. The backdrop of mass shootings has marked how Generation Zers view the spaces they spend time in and what safety means in relative terms. For Jewish Generation Zers with regard to physical safety, the Tree of Life shooting was more of the same. They are used to being aware of the potential vulnerabilities that they face in the institutions that they occupy. For many, what made the Tree of Life shooting unique was the aftermath, rather than the act itself.

Bailey acknowledged a sense of feeling irrational with regard to the disparity between the reactions of the Jewish community and the rest of the population in response to antisemitism in the United States. "The lack of response from people outside the Jewish community . . . sometimes it feels like you're being gaslit,[13] and you end up asking, 'Am I taking this too seriously, because only my community is reacting?'" Rebecca, from Texas, echoed the feeling of isolation that came from the lack of reaction from individuals outside of the Jewish community. "Jews helping Jews is protecting your own, but we need to have other people who care." Amanda Berman, the Zioness founder and executive director, outlined the difference between what others are *obligated* to do and what ideally *should* have happened. "I don't demand that if I show up for someone, they show up for me. Allyship is not a quid pro quo. But if someone does care about justice, they should care about Jews."

Lisa works with teachers in public schools who teach the Holocaust, generally as part of social studies or literature courses. The pedagogical framework of her organization's approach centers around the use of intellectual rigor and emotional engagement to help students think about the respective choices that they each make on a daily basis. "It's not 'What would I have done if I was in Auschwitz or something,' but more 'Where in my daily life do I see my community dividing into we/they situations, where are people othered, and then what choices do I make based on that?'" The pedagogic approach of her organization is meant to instill allyship between groups who otherwise would likely be inclined to be isolated from one another, a reality all too frequent, even in an ever-increasingly diverse United States. Lisa noted, "Teens live in hyper-segregated spaces, so they're not exposed to others without even realizing it. I'll get a lot of questions: 'If people live where they want to live, and Black people want to live near Black people or Jewish people want to live near Jewish people, what's the problem?'"

Squirrel Hill is known for being one of Pittsburgh's Jewish population centers. In 2010, approximately 40 percent of Squirrel Hill's residents were Jewish,[14] with an earlier population study of the Pittsburgh Jewish community reporting that nearly 50 percent of the local Jewish community lived in Squirrel Hill and its surrounding neighborhoods.[15] The shooting, so clearly focused on the Jewish community, could easily have remained an internal issue, and indeed, the outpouring of grief from Jewish communities around the world was widespread and all-encompassing for many. But it also created a ripple effect outside of the local community and the Jewish community, inspiring acts of solidarity and allyship from everyone from the Pittsburgh Steelers[16] to an Iranian graduate student in Washington, DC, who launched a GoFundMe campaign that raised over $1 million in donations for the victims.[17]

The Tree of Life shooting, by virtue of its status as the deadliest attack on the American Jewish community, is unique. But in other ways, particularly in its aftermath, it has become another line on an ever-growing list of mass-casualty shootings that have permeated and then faded in the collective American consciousness. One year after the shooting, Emma Green wrote in *The Atlantic*, "As after other mass shootings in America . . . with each anniversary, the Pittsburgh attack will slip further into the great fog of forgetting, swallowed up by the latest national political drama or by workaday life. Yesterday, Pittsburgh's Jewish community marked one year since the deadliest anti-Semitic attack on U.S. soil. This morning, they still woke up with their grief, while America largely continued to move on."[18] It is, of course, human nature to move forward, with past events fading into the recesses of collective memory. But for an incident that became as much of a landmark event, as the Tree of Life shooting has been for the American Jewish community, to fade so quickly creates a disconnect between Jews coming of age in its wake and their peers.

Emma Green continued, "Over the past year, I have met dozens of Jewish college students from across the country at conferences and student-journalism events. Invariably, conversations turn to the shooting, and, invariably, at least one student starts crying, remembering how isolated she felt on campus after the attack or how much her sense of security has been shaken. For some American Jews, especially young people, this shooting may have been their first encounter with deadly anti-Semitism, and their first experience questioning their safety as Jews."

The Pittsburgh shooting brought to a head the lived contradictions that many American Jews experience, often unconsciously. "Modern Jewish life in America is premised on an unusual duality. On the one hand, we are a historically persecuted minority, imbued with a deep post-Holocaust sense of insecurity. On the other hand, the average Jew enjoys tremendous privilege in America—we are typically wealthier than the average Americans, and overrepresented in nearly every prestigious career and industry. This is a testament to how safe the United States has been for us."[19] There is no question that the United States, despite never eradicating antisemitism, has been a backdrop against which the Jewish community has been able to thrive. At the same time, the antisemitism that has existed as an undercurrent that boiled over in Pittsburgh in October 2018 has shaped the psyches of generations of American Jews.

Brad noted, "When you're the target of antisemitism and you grow up in an environment with pervasive antisemitic conditioning that impacts every aspect of society, it's going to become internalized to varying degrees. It's going to have an impact on your sense of self, confidence, perception of worthiness, and perception of capacity to thrive in certain environments." In many ways, the shooting at Tree of Life irreparably shattered a degree of innocence in the American Jewish collective psyche. Young Jews have felt what it is to be targets, and to know that yet another previously safe space for them, like schools, nightclubs, and other gathering spaces, could not be seen as inherently safe and secure.

Research indicates that exposure to violence in the local environment, whether direct or indirect, has harmful effects on young people's brain architecture at a critical time in their development. It can also lead to a variety of mental health challenges, including post-traumatic stress and children and youth having difficulty self-regulating their behavior.[20] While the majority of American Jews do not live in Pittsburgh, nor were they in close proximity, either geographically or via direct family ties, the bonds of Jewish peoplehood[21] created a reality wherein the shooting and its aftermath became personal despite these boundaries. And indeed, the sense of safety—a concept that unites the objective risk of being involved in an act of aggression, an individual's perception of that risk, and their personal assessment of vulnerability[22]—of Jews nationwide were impacted. Dina, the mother of two Generation Zers in the Washington, DC, area, noted the mindset shifts that occurred in the aftermath of the attack. "The world became a scary place. Not that it wasn't scary before, but now, everything is more out there."

The shooting changed how Jewish institutions are viewed and choices are made. A few reactions from Generation Zers in the aftermath of the attack:

"Our synagogue is set back from the road and doesn't have any visible signage. I'm glad we don't have to worry about people knowing who we are as easily."

"I'm not going to let them take away my identity."

"My family goes to synagogue every week. But after the shooting, my mom told me I couldn't hang out in the lobby with the other kids anymore."

"I feel comfortable being Jewish. But I'm definitely aware of what I say where and who's around if I'm talking about it."

"At camp we used to have all of these activities where we had to say if we felt like Jewish Americans or American Jews. That's not productive. We're American and Jewish, and a shooter can't take that away from us."

In the weeks after the shooting at Tree of Life–Or L'Simcha Congregation in 2018, I felt called to journey to Pittsburgh and to see what remained for myself. So I drove, together with the friends that once made that city a home for me, to stand in the shadows of death and of life. We arrived at twilight and parked on a street corner that only weeks before had been unremarkable. Squirrel Hill is a neighborhood that's at once busy and peaceful. The homes are graceful and the people are friendly. There's a regular hum of traffic and activity, with plenty of foot traffic and waves exchanged between neighbors and strangers alike. It's the kind of place where even if you don't know anyone, you'll get smiles and head nods on every block.

But in the late fall of 2018, the streets seemed oddly hushed. The air itself hung heavy, and the corner lot that held the synagogue was foreboding, with police tape left over and makeshift memorial items piled against the glass doors. My friends and I gathered on the steps outside the front doors, which have been locked ever since the day of the shooting. Inside, there were overflowing memorial items: flowers, notes, Stars of David with the names of the victims. As we stood in silence, others stopped by as well—mourners, seekers, gawkers—people who were drawn to that place at that time. The feeling I remember the most is numbness. No tears, even though my heart broke thinking of the lives lost. No anger, even though in moments before and after, I found myself overcome with a sense of incredulous rage about how this happened. Not even fear, standing exposed under the night sky. But rather a cold knot of hopelessness, and uncertainty at how to move forward when the world was now so clearly divided into the time before and the time after the attack.

I left Squirrel Hill that evening, unsure of what would be different but sure that things would be. I didn't return to the site of the shooting for nearly two years. I drove different routes when I went to Pittsburgh otherwise, not wanting the building and its memorial to fade into the background but not ready to mark the time and space. When I did return, it was in the company of fifty teens from Cleveland, who made a pilgrimage to Tree of Life–Or L'Simcha Congregation as part of a conference focused on antisemitism and intolerance. By then, the synagogue doors were still locked, and the building was encircled by art panels designed and sent by students from around the world. The majority of the panels came from students in Parkland, Florida, who felt connected to the synagogue as members of the club no one wants to be part of: those living with emotional scars of surviving a mass shooting.

My students met with congregants from the synagogues that were attacked, who were able to share stories of the friends that they lost. They met with a former self-described white supremacist and violent extremist who has since transformed into an educator and community shaper.[23] And they gathered together outside of the doors of the synagogue, taking in the memorial objects I had seen two years before, and raised their voices in song. We said the Mourner's Kaddish[24] for the victims, and sang the Hatikvah[25] as an expression of hope.

In some ways, it was awkward. While Generation Zers have been shaped by mass shootings and are able to be solemn in their aftermaths, there is still a tendency to be unsure about how to behave in the face of loss, of trauma, of hate. At this moment, on top of all of the awkwardness of adolescence, it was also personal. "I could have been here that day. You're not as far away or as immune as you might want to think. It could easily happen in my synagogue too." Jaime, then a high school junior, shared this sense of connection, which was echoed by many of her peers. Generation Zers are in consensus: Pittsburgh, and the Tree of Life–Or L'Simcha Congregation were the targets this time. But it's understood, whether on the surface or as an innate knowledge from within, that next time is a question of when and not if, and that any community could be the next in line.

NOTES

1. Brown, R. (2020, January 22). Poland is in denial about its role in the Holocaust: It was both victim and perpetrator. *Independent*. Retrieved from https://www.independent.co.uk/voices/poland-holocaust-denial-anti semitism-ambassador-arkady-rzegocki-a9297106.html

2. Vagianos, A. (2018, March 19). Parkland students: "We're the mass shooting generation." HuffPost. Retrieved from https://www.huffpost .com/entry/parkland-students-were-the-mass-shooting-generation_n_5aaf b06be4b0337adf85a6a4

3. Greenberg, B. (n.d.). Why Jews hang a mezuzah on the doorpost. My Jewish Learning. Retrieved from https://www.myjewishlearning.com/arti cle/mezuzah

4. My Jewish Learning (n.d.). Chanukiah. Retrieved from https://www .myjewishlearning.com/article/chanukiah

5. https://www.genzjews.com

6. Desmond-Harris, J. (2015, February 16). What exactly is a microaggression? Vox. Retrieved from https://www.vox.com/2015/2/16/8031073 /what-are-microaggressions

7. Gessen, M. (2018, October 27). Why the tree of life shooter was fixated on the Hebrew immigrant aid society. *New Yorker*. Retrieved from https://www.newyorker.com/news/our-columnists/why-the-tree-of-life -shooter-was-fixated-on-the-hebrew-immigrant-aid-society

8. Ward, P. R., Lord, R., & Navatril, L. (2018, October 27). Suspect identified as Robert Bowers, 46, in Squirrel Hill synagogue shooting. *Pittsburgh Post-Gazette*.

9. Goldstein, A. (2018, November 9). Eighty years after Kristallnacht, glass again shatters in the Jewish community. *Pittsburgh Post-Gazette*. Retrieved from https://www.post-gazette.com/local/city/2018/11/09/kristall nacht-events-pittsburgh-tree-of-life-anniversary-novemeber-9-10-byham -nazi/stories/201811070195

10. Garbell, C. (2018, November 8). After Tree of Life attack, don't tell Jews all hate crimes & bigoted attacks are the same. *USA Today*. Retrieved from https://www.usatoday.com/story/opinion/voices/2018/11/08/jews-anti -semitism-shooting-pittsburgh-europe-hate-crime-column/1890066002

11. Robinson, M., & Gould, S. (2018, December 31). There were 340 mass shootings in the US in 2018: Here's the full list. *Business Insider*. Retrieved from https://www.businessinsider.com/how-many-mass-shootings -in-america-this-year-2018-2

12. American Psychological Association (2018, October). Stress in America: Generation Z. Retrieved from https://www.apa.org/news/press /releases/stress/2018/stress-gen-z.pdf

13. Huizen, J. (2020, July 14). What is gaslighting? *Medical News Today*. Retrieved from https://www.medicalnewstoday.com/articles/gas lighting

14. Ansberry, C. (2010, July 2). Diverse views on Israel emerge in Jewish enclave. *Wall Street Journal*. Retrieved from https://www.wsj.com /articles/SB10001424052748703374104575336692368479502?mod= rss_middle_east_news

15. The 2002 Pittsburgh Jewish Community Study.

16. Jonas, M. (2018, October 28). Steelers hold moment of silence for Pittsburgh synagogue shooting victims. *USA Today*.

17. Rotstein, G. (2018, November 1). Iranian raised $1 million for Tree of Life, gets showered with offers of Steelers, Penguins tickets. *Pittsburgh Post-Gazette*.

18. Green, E. (2019, October 28). America has already forgotten the Tree of Life shooting. *The Atlantic*. Retrieved from https://www.theatlan tic.com/politics/archive/2019/10/tree-life-and-legacy-pittsburghs-syna gogue-attack/600946

19. Beauchamp, Z. (2019, October 25). How the Pittsburgh shooting changed American Jews. Vox. Retrieved from https://www.vox.com/the -highlight/2019/10/18/20899208/tree-of-life-anniversary-pittsburgh-shooting -american-jews

20. Center for Promise (2018, February). When youth feel unsafe: Brief insights on the cognitive and academic effects of exposure to violence. Retrieved from https://files.eric.ed.gov/fulltext/ED586283.pdf

21. Peoplehood Now. NADAV Foundation.

22. Migliorini, L., Rania, N., Cardinali, P., & Manetti, M. (2008). Sense of safety and the urban environment: A study of preadolescents and adolescents. *Medio Ambiente y Comportamiento Humano, 9*, pp. 69–89.

23. Shannon Foley Martinez, https://www.shannonmartinezspeaks.com

24. My Jewish Learning (n.d.). Text of the mourner's kaddish. Retrieved from   https://www.myjewishlearning.com/article/text-of-the-mourners-kaddish

25. My Jewish Learning (n.d.). Hatikvah, the national anthem of Israel. Retrieved from https://www.myjewishlearning.com/article/national-anthem-of-israel

FIVE

The Dyke March: How Anti-Israelism Becomes Antisemitism

As a college freshman, I lived in a dorm known as The Towers, where each floor had communal bathrooms shared by forty other students. It's there that I learned the unique art of bathroom small talk, the casual conversations and murmurings used to fill silences of people you shared intimacies with but otherwise were not likely to speak with regularly. Usually, these conversations were limited to banal exchanges about class schedules and the weather. But on one occasion, a floormate I hadn't spoken to except for some icebreakers back during welcome week popped up at the next sink with this opening question: "You're Jewish, right?" After I responded in the affirmative, the immediate follow-up came. "How can you stand what *you people* are doing to the Palestinians?"

Margot, the parent of two Generation Z–aged daughters in Kentucky, dreads just this sort of experience for her children. "I want Judaism to be easier for them. I don't want my daughter to arrive on campus and someone to ask her about Israel and for her to have a deer-in-the-headlights reaction. I want her to feel comfortable holding the reality of the situation and its complexities. I think that they feel ready for those conversations, but we won't really know until we get there."

In terms of the supposed dichotomy of being pro-Israel versus being pro-Palestinian that my floormate espoused, Amanda Berman, the founder and executive director of Zioness, rejects the all-too-common belief that supporting Israel and supporting the Palestinian people are concepts in conflict with one another. "I hope people don't fall for the false binary that if you care about Palestinians, you have to hate Israel." What she struggles with is the aggression that comes as part of the package for an increasing number of people and groups that engage in antinormalization, which involves refusing to interact with Israelis and supporters in Israel—namely, Jews.[1] "People are living in an alternate reality where they refuse to speak to people who believe Israel exists and has the *right* to exist. In reality, that means you're effectively refusing to speak to the majority of Jews. How is that not antisemitism?"

For many American Jews, coming of age too often means being called upon to explain, defend, or even justify the actions and legitimacy of the State of Israel. I came of age during the Second Intifada and its aftermath. It was a time when mentioning Israel conjured images of bus bombings and suicide attacks and the controversy of the then-in-progress security fence[2] that then–prime minister Ariel Sharon began constructing around the perimeters of the West Bank. The conversations that I had about Israel as an emerging adult largely came through the lens of being an advocate. As a proud Zionist and aspiring activist, I felt a deep responsibility to clarify misconceptions, counter misinformation, and generally show up "loud and proud" to demonstrate my love and support for Israel. I was armed with facts, personal lived experiences, and the passion that comes from a commitment and connection to a cause beyond oneself. Mara, the freshman at Binghamton University, is also well versed in Israel advocacy and the instilled belief that one of her roles as an American Jew is to be a voice for Israel.

"I don't know how early it came up, but it was made clear really early on that we should have a fear that one day, we won't be welcome in America anymore, and we'll have to go to Israel. I remember my third-grade teacher telling us that we might like it here in America, and we might feel safe, but one day we would no longer be welcome and we would need to go to Israel. We were nine years old."

Amanda Berman identified that mindset as one that is not necessarily typical for Generation Zers to inherit. "We live in a world right now where the majority of American Jews have only lived in a world where Israel has existed. So there's a total naivete about the extent of Jewish vulnerability. I say this as a compliment to Jewish institutions, who have been so successful in making sure that the Jewish community is integrated, engaged, has a voice, organizes, etc. The fact that we *don't* understand vulnerability means that someone has done a great job of making us safe."

Regardless of which school of thought one falls under in their personal lived experiences, it is understood that the American Jewish experience is marked by Israel. Whether it's the presence or the absence of Israel in Jewish spaces, conversations, and prayers, or the emphasis on Israel education, to come of age in the Jewish community is to at some point encounter Israel. For the majority of Generation Zers coming of age, at some point in their lives, they have or will be asked to be in relationship with the people, state, and land of Israel. Whether it's by fellow Jewish community insiders, who work to ensure that Generation Zers care about Israel and see it as critical to connect them with it as part of the cultivation of their overall Jewish identities, or by detractors, who will call into question how Israel and American Jews intersect, Israel is a consistent presence in the American Jewish landscape. Arielle, the Instagram content creator from Connecticut whom we met earlier, expressed her frustration with the status quo. "I don't like that as soon as someone hears that you're Jewish, they automatically bring up Israel. They're not one and the same, but they're not fully separate either. . . . I identify as pro-peace. I think pro-Israel and pro-Palestinian is a false dichotomy." And at this particular juncture, the issue of Israel has been weaponized by both the Left and the Right as a tool of antisemitic rhetoric and actions. For a generation of American Jews who are largely liberal, culturally affiliated, and concerned about allyship, the complexities of Israel have often led to confusion and even disillusionment.

The modern State of Israel was established in 1948, against a backdrop of war and controversy from its inception. Israel has long been the historic national homeland of the Jewish people, and in the years following the end of World War II and the aftermath of the Holocaust, the Zionist cause that had existed for generations gained traction on the world's stage. On November 29, 1947, the League of Nations voted in favor of the partition of the land then known as the British Mandate of Palestine into two entities: a Jewish state and an Arab state. While the provisional government of the Jewish state accepted the imperfect partition agreement, the Arab nations rejected it, leading to a war from the day of Israel declaring its independence on May 14, 1948. The subsequent bloodshed, known to Israelis as the War of Independence and the Arabs as the *Nakhba* ["catastrophe"], ended with a tenuous new reality: a Jewish state and displaced Arabs who became the core of the Palestinian refugee population.[3]

Since 1948, Israel has fought numerous wars with its Arab neighbors, and while it has continued to establish itself among the community of nations, never has it been fully accepted by the global community. While for Israelis, the majority of Jews, and much of the world, the reality of

Israel is a nonissue, there is a pervasive undercurrent of detractors who question the right of Israel to exist as an independent country. In the United States, Israel, which was once a unifying issue for the Jewish community and both sides of the aisle politically, has become an increasingly emotionally charged and polarizing subject. From both the political and ideological Left and Right, the State of Israel and the reality of its existence have been weaponized as a tool of antisemitic rhetoric.

Bailey, the college student from North Carolina, reflected on the increasingly polarizing role of Israel, particularly when it comes to setting boundaries within the Jewish community. "Jewish life has become a politicized space relating to the Israeli-Palestinian conflict, and there are Jewish students who don't feel comfortable as a result of that. There's a Jewish community that's obvious on campus, and a Jewish community beyond that that's frequently neglected. Many Jewish spaces, instead of being spaces for *Judaism,* have become these places of volatile political discourse. So people are left out of what could be a healing space in certain situations."

Bailey shared her experience with the antisemitic rhetoric of TikTok. In her experience, this kind of ubiquitous outburst is directly linked to bias centered around Israel. "A Jewish TikTok will be posted, and it'll have nothing related to Israel. But immediately in the comments there'll be flags of Israel, or Palestine, just as a response to Jewish content. We live in a world where they've become so meshed together, but for me it's easy to separate my Judaism from the state of Israel." Blythe has given voice to multiple realities. On social media, as well as in "real life," Judaism and the State of Israel are often viewed as synonymous. For someone spreading anti-Israel rhetoric, there is often no differentiation between Judaism and Israel. All too often, Generation Zers who are turning to social media to express pride in their Jewish identities are hit with a barrage of anti-Israel sentiments, attempting to shut down their attempts at self-expression. From both the Left and the Right, Israel is increasingly used as a barometer for acceptance of Jews.

Rebecca, the Texan-turned–University of Oklahoma student, reflected on her perceptions about how Israel factors into her experience. "I think the feeling that you need to check your Israel self is more of a subconscious or self-conscious thing for most people—because we want to fit in, and sometimes being passionate about Israel can keep you on the outside of things. I found that in high school I felt like I needed to hide my Judaism, or at least to hide the opinions that a Jew has." Mara further reflected,

"I've never felt that my Judaism is exactly a liability to my progressiveness, but I hear my peers say it all the time."

Amanda Berman, as noted earlier, heads the Zioness Movement, an initiative dedicated to empowering and activating Zionists on the progressive left to stand proudly in social justice spaces as Jews and Zionists. An attorney by training, Amanda was inspired to spearhead Zioness in late 2017, as a result of grappling with feelings of isolation from the progressive movement because of her commitment to Zionism,[4] and she sought to build a space dedicated to the synergy between her Zionist and progressive values. Zioness, which describes itself as a coalition of Jewish activists and allies who are unabashedly progressive and unapologetically Zionist, has chapters in twenty states and reaches Zionist allies and activists nationwide. For Amanda, the idea of anti-Israel sentiment being wholly different from antisemitism is incongruous. "If you oppose the existence of one state in the whole world and it happens to be the Jewish state, you have an antisemitism problem."

Zionism, by definition, is the national movement for the return of the Jewish people to their homeland [the land of Israel] and the resumption of sovereignty [self-determination] for the Jewish people.[5] Zionism has manifested in different ways from before the establishment of the State of Israel and up until its twenty-first-century connotations and schools of thought. However, the overarching belief in the right of the Jewish people to self-determination has of late become a flashpoint of controversy across the political aisle. While all sovereign countries are subject to criticism, both internally and externally, and Israel is no different, scholars and activists have sought to delineate when legitimate criticism of Israel lapses into antisemitism.

Natan Sharansky, Israeli politician and thought leader, developed a metric for testing whether or not criticism of Israel qualifies as antisemitism. The test, known as the 3D test, is outlined as:

Delegitimization of Israel

Demonization of Israel

Subjecting Israel to **D**ouble standards[6]

Sharansky developed this concept in 2003, during his time as a minister in the Israeli government. Subsequently, the test was adopted by the U.S. Department of State in 2010,[7] though it was later replaced by the Working Definition of Antisemitism in 2017. The 3D test has been endorsed by

Israeli, American, and global Jewish leaders and educators. As it stands, each of the three Ds is an often-used tactic of anti-Israel detractors, who are not interested in legitimately criticizing Israeli policies and actions but, rather, call into question the fundamental right of the state to exist at all. Amanda's response to individuals who call Israel's existence into question is simple. "Every people should have sovereignty. That's what we strive for as progressives. So if you believe in states, and borders in general, and you want a Palestinian state, you should also believe in a Jewish state. When people say 'I'm a progressive so I'm anti-Israel,' I say, 'So do you want to return the Jews to a state of total powerlessness?'"

Each of the three Ds is a modern manifestation of antisemitism. Delegitimization of Israel refers to the denial of the right of the Jewish people to self-determination by, for example, claiming that the State of Israel is an innately racist endeavor. It discriminates against the Jewish people by singling them out as being ineligible for the basic right of self-determination.[8] Demonization is a new iteration of the ancient blood libels that have been tools of antisemitism for generations. Antisemitism often charges Jews with conspiring to harm humanity,[9] and this rhetoric has been applied to the State of Israel as a corollary with the Jewish people. It manifests as portraying Israel and Israelis as inhuman or as controllers of the media, economy, government, or other global and societal institutions.[10] Finally, double standards refer to the application of differing standards and sets of principles for similar situations and to not judging Israel according to the same metrics as the rest of the global community is judged. This argument states that if people who criticize Israel, and only Israel, on certain issues but ignore similar situations in other countries, they are using a double standard to single out the Jewish state. By applying a different moral standard to Israel alone, the charge is that detractors are discriminating against the Jewish State and are engaging in antisemitism.[11] Amanda Berman summed up double standards succinctly. "Criticizing Israeli policy looks like criticizing Israeli policy. Not demonizing Jewish people who support Israel."

Ella, the high school student from Los Angeles whom we met earlier, had her own experience with double standards as a manifestation of antisemitism. She previously spearheaded the launch of a constitutional debate club at her high school, a process that was rubber-stamped as ordinary and quickly approved by the administration. However, when it came time to go through the process of starting an Israel club, she noted that the whole process felt different. This time around, the administration required a safety plan, a written club constitution, and numerous other bureaucratic hoops to be jumped through. While none of the policies made for the Israel club in particular was egregious or unreasonable, putting extra restrictions on this organization that others did not have is a micro example of the double standards regularly faced by Israel, and, by association, by its Jewish supporters around the world.

Adam, whom we also met earlier, gave voice to the double standard applied to Jewish progressives when it comes to the Israeli Palestinian conflict. "Needing to qualify that I'm Jewish but I'm also against the oppression of the Palestinian people is internalized racism *and* internalized antisemitism. When we say things like that, we think we're getting ahead of the perception of who we are so others won't sort us into a 'good' or 'bad' category."

When it comes to conversations about Israel, what it means to be a "good" Jew manifests differently depending on the space that one is in. While the majority of American Jews, and Americans as a whole, continue to support Israel,[12] there are certain ideological places where said support is thought to be contradictory to other liberal, progressive values. In the 2000s, several watershed moments took place that became flashpoints of how Zionism and the progressive Left are seen as at odds with one another. This is despite what many Jews and non-Jewish supporters of Israel see as inherently shared values between the Zionist and progressive movements. In *Jewish Pride,* Ben M. Freeman wrote, "Zionism is nothing but the movement to return an ethno-religious minority, a nation and a people, to their indigenous homeland, which should perfectly align with progressive values." But despite this sense that Zionism should be seen as ideologically connected to liberal and progressive movements, the facts on the ground have proved different.

Beginning in 1993, Dyke Marches have been held in cities around the world. A Dyke March is defined as a lesbian visibility and protest march, with the goal of encouraging activism within the lesbian community. Dyke Marches are most often held during the month of June as part of Pride celebrations and are important events for lesbian communities as well as the larger LGBTQ+ community and their allies. However, in several instances, Jewish marchers have been targeted, discriminated against, and ultimately barred from participation in these events.

In 2017, the organizers of Chicago's Dyke March singled out three women carrying Jewish Pride flags. The marchers were asked questions about their views on Israel and their relationships with Zionism and were ultimately asked to leave the event. The organizers held that by waving rainbow flags with the Star of David emblem on them, the Jewish marchers were making people feel unsafe. They stated that ideologically, the Dyke March was pro-Palestinian and anti-Zionist.[13] Subsequently, in 2019, the Washington, DC, Dyke March adopted a policy that banned the display of "nationalist symbols," including Israeli and American flags, as well as the Star of David when centered on flags.[14] The justification behind such policies is that these symbols represent "violent nationalism." At the same time, other identifications of Judaism and Jewishness, including yarmulkes and tallitot, as well as Palestinian flags and symbols, were permitted.[15]

New School undergraduate Rafaella Gunz reflected on this double standard:

> Since 2017, when Jewish lesbians were asked to leave the annual Chicago Dyke March because their Pride flags featuring the Star of David were deemed "Zionist," I saw the veiled anti-Semitism bubbling up on the left. Why were American Jews being asked to leave a Pride event because of the actions of a country of which they're not citizens? I couldn't imagine anyone kicking out Muslims if their Pride flag featured the crescent moon symbol, which is on the flags of many countries criticized for human-rights abuses, including Turkey, Libya and Pakistan. I had enough common sense to recognize not all Muslims are connected to those nations or blindly endorse the politics of those countries. Likewise, I couldn't blindly endorse the politics of those countries. Likewise, I couldn't see the organization kicking out Christians with a cross on their Pride flag, despite Christian imagery on the flags of nations such as the UK, Norway, Sweden and Finland.[16]

By policing which expressions of Jewish identity are permitted and encouraged in this progressive space, and by limiting identifying markers connected to Jewish nationalism, the organizers of these marches are effectively delineating what forms of Judaism are acceptable. Zionism at its core is a movement that aims to return a historically oppressed people to their indigenous homeland, giving them self-determination after generations of exile, ethnic cleansing, and ultimately genocide. And yet, LGBTQ Jews, as well as allies within the Jewish community, are being asked to choose between their various identities and are being told that how they express their Judaism is not in line with the values of this other core community that they are inherently part of. Being required to choose between self-determination as Jews and as members of the LGBTQ community is effectively suppressing the identity of a minority group and its rights.

This kind of movement-sanctioned suppression is not limited to the LGBTQ community. The Women's March, which began as a worldwide protest the day after the inauguration of President Donald Trump, was the largest single-day protest in U.S. history. For thousands of women, as well as male allies, around the United States and the world, the Women's March became a rallying point. After hearing anti-women remarks from President Trump, joining together to advocate for women's rights as human rights instilled pride and a spirit of activism throughout communities.[17] The Washington march alone drew over 470,000 people, with worldwide participation estimated at over 7 million. The march movement was seen as successful, and plans were made for a subsequent gathering the following year.

However, accusations quickly began spreading of antisemitic rhetoric within the Women's March, with three of the cochairs being called out by Bari Weiss, then-columnist for the *New York Times,* for their continued associations with Louis Farrakhan and for failing to reject antisemitism.[18] By the time the 2019 March was being organized, there were calls for cochairs Linda Sarsour, Tamika Mallory, Bob Bland, and Carmen Perez to resign. It was found that in February 2018, Mallory had attended an event with Nation of Islam leader Louis Farrakhan, where he referenced "Satanic Jews."[19] Linda Sarsour responded to the accusations of antisemitism, flipping the script and alleging that the criticisms came because of her opposition to Israel.[20] Though she eventually condemned the antisemitism within the march community, a great deal of damage was done. Sarsour had already stated, "It just doesn't make any sense for someone to say, 'Is there room for people who support the state of Israel and do not criticize it in the [feminist] movement?' There can't be in feminism. You either stand up for the rights of all women, including Palestinians, or none. There's just no way around it."[21]

At the time of the 2020 Women's March, Jewish journalist Emily Shire wrote, "Jewish women who voiced even an iota of qualified support for Israel were met with hostility, but that didn't only affect Zionists. By effectively forcing Jewish women to prove that they didn't support Israel, *all* Jewish women got the message that our acceptance was qualified and conditional."[22]

The Dyke March and the Women's March are only two examples of how the progressive movement has used Israel as a proxy for antisemitic sentiment and rhetoric. On college campuses, in high school clubs, and in liberal spaces that deeply align with their Jewish values, Jews are asked, either implicitly or even explicitly, to denounce or disassociate themselves from Israel in order to be accepted as progressives. And in a reality where their progressive values are often what drives them, Jewishly and otherwise, asking Generation Zers to make this choice sets up questions, heartbreak, and disconnect.

David, the father of a high school senior and an eighth grader in Missouri, acknowledges that at this moment, his children feel comfortable being Jewish. While they are used to being in minority roles, often being the only Jews in whatever room they're in, they have found ways to balance their Judaism with their broader intersectional identities. Ironically, COVID-19 helped in this endeavor, with his varsity athlete child, who otherwise would have had to opt out of participation in synagogue activities, finding new opportunities to connect by Zooming into social and learning sessions. As David's older child prepares to enter university, there are familial concerns that by leaving the comfort of home, Israel will become a contentious issue rather than one of pride. "My son is planning to major in environmental studies. I worry that as he gravitates toward more left-leaning circles, he'll have a hard time managing. Things are quiet now, but you never know how long that'll last. So we're watching out for it."

There is an awareness of the difference between antisemitism and other forms of discrimination, particularly when it comes to the attitudes of young people. While other forms of prejudice are less popular among younger generations, which tend to be more tolerant, research has shown that antisemitic attitudes are consistently higher for this same demographic.[23] This same survey has shown that young conservatives are more likely than young liberals to believe stereotypes about Jews, but young liberals are the most likely to hold Jews responsible for Israel's actions. The survey, conducted by Tufts University professor Eitan Hersh and Harvard doctoral student Laura Ryoden, was designed "with particular sensitivity to the public conversations about the relationship between anti-Israel activities and antisemitism." The researchers went on to note, "While we find evidence consistent with theories of both left-wing and right-wing antisemitism, the results convey an unambiguous message that antisemitic attitudes are far more prevalent on the right. In addition, our evidence suggests significantly higher rates of antisemitic attitudes among racial minorities relative to whites across the ideological spectrum."

College campuses are known as being spaces of high activity as it relates to the Israeli-Palestinian conflict, which is thought to contribute to the feeling that Israel and Jews may be viewed as oppressors by many young adults in a way that previous generations did not experience.[24] While at other moments in history, Israel was seen as the more sympathetic party in its conflicts with its Arab neighbors, today, that is no longer the case, particularly among young progressives.[25] Instead, support for Palestinians and criticism of Israel have become the predominant trend in many progressive movements.[26]

While criticism of Israel can be legitimate and does not automatically fall into the category of antisemitism, negative attitudes about Israel can often lead to antisemitic sentiments: "To the extent that liberal identifiers seek to identify with the oppressed over the oppressor and believe that Israel is an oppressor, they might hold negative attitudes towards Jews, who they associate with the oppressor. Just as progressives might express dislike toward evangelical Christians if they identify evangelical Christians as a group that holds a set of policy views they deem oppressive (e.g., anti-LGBTQ), progressives might similarly dislike Jews as group for holding a set of pro-Israel views they deem to be oppressive."[27]

For many parents of Generation Zers, Israel is a source of concern on a variety of levels. Dina, the mother of two college-aged Generation Zers, values giving her children the opportunity to engage with Judaism on their own terms. But when it comes to Israel, additional questions arise. "As the kids try to figure out their own Jewish voices, they defend Israel. But they don't agree with all of its policies. They may actually agree with their friends who are criticizing Israel, but how do they do that in a Jewish way?" Jeff, whose Generation Zers have not yet entered college, is holding his breath regarding what they may face. "Of course, I'm worried about what connection they're going to have with Israel. We [Jewish institutions and leaders] need to really listen and figure out what they need in terms of Israel. We're still teaching love at any cost and hiding realities. Once they have the opportunity to question and explore on their own, if they think they were misled, they'll turn their backs."

For years, college campuses have been seen as the front lines in the proverbial battle for hearts and minds as it relates to opinions on Israel. Jewish organizations, leaders, and individuals have invested significant amounts of time, resources, and emotional capital in preparing and training incoming and current students on responding to attacks against Israel, and, by association, against them as Jews. But despite this investment, there is still a sense, for many Jewish Generation Zers as well as their parents, that they are unprepared to encounter anti-Israel sentiments that are so increasingly found on college campuses.[28]

Melinda, the mother of a Generation Z middle schooler, noted the generational difference currently being experienced. "Growing up, it felt like there was more moral clarity. I knew that I was Jewish, and therefore what my values were. And now things are a lot more ambiguous, and a lot of that is Israel. No matter what you say, it's toxic to a key part of your community. Generation Z as a whole will probably be afraid to explore what they believe and to do research or to take an unpopular stance within their social groups. We're moving toward more polarization with Israel and young Jews. Going to Israel isn't enough. It's something, and it shows complexity, but there has to be more."

Meghan is the mother of three Generation Zers. She lives in Virginia and has two children in college out of state and one still at home. Their family was always connected with Israel and went on a few family trips while her kids were growing up. In ways that were intentional, and others that were decidedly unintentional, the children were raised with strong Jewish identities that were enhanced by the experience of being minorities. Her eldest child is a student at a large midwestern university and chose her school based in part on the comfort of having a Jewish community while not feeling the need to be "in the bubble" and to fully surround herself with exclusively Jewish peers. Upon arriving on campus, she started getting involved Jewishly, through the campus Hillel.

"[She] started hosting dinners for friends on holidays, and loved it," Meghan stated. "And then she became the de-facto leader of JStreet [a progressive Zionist group] on campus. I worry about her personal safety sometimes. Hillel is a very obvious looking building, and I know that in some parts of the country, we do look different. Even without stars on or anything, we do seem Jewish, and I have to wonder if that's a good thing."

Meaningfully encountering Israel often proves to be a watershed movement for young Jews. For some, their first intensive Israel experiences, whether they're positive or negative, have the potential to change the trajectory of their Jewish stories. For Rafaella Gunz, like many of her peers, encountering anti-Israel sentiments spurred her to action. After a series of negative interactions with the Students for Justice in Palestine chapter at her law school, Rafaella began to embrace Zionism. "Lately, I've discovered the term 'Zionism' is much like the term 'feminism,' insofar as it's divisive and has different meanings to different people. Ask a Men's Rights activist what he thinks feminism means and you'll likely be told it's about 'female supremacy' as opposed to what it actually is: gender equality. Ask most Western social justice activists what Zionism means, you'll likely be told it means 'Jewish supremacy and the oppression of Palestinians.' In fact, it simply means the right for Jewish self-determination in their indigenous, ancestral homeland."[29]

It has been said that antisemitism is not, in fact, a Jewish problem. Rather, it is a problem for non-Jews that ultimately impacts Jews. But while the majority of antisemitism is in fact directed either at Jews or at those perceived to be Jewish, particularly as it pertains to Israel, there is an additional undercurrent of internalized antisemitism that manifests in the idea of the "self-hating Jew." This term has been used in a number of contexts throughout history in order to describe Jews whose own views or actions align with antisemitic sentiments and has also been referred to as auto-antisemitism. The most common usage of this term tends to come in circumstances related to Israel. It's a controversial stance to take. In a reflection on the topic from *My Jewish Learning,* it's noted that "some scholars have claimed that by labeling another Jew self-hating, the accuser is claiming his or her own Judaism as normative—and implying that the Judaism of the accused is flawed or incorrect, based on a metric of the accuser's own stances, religious beliefs, or political opinions."[30]

Accusing another of self-hatred is a designation that assumes some degree of authority about whose opinions count as within acceptable boundaries. But when complex feelings are raised within the Jewish community as it pertains to Israel, sometimes it can feel like all bets are off. Bailey, the college student from North Carolina, noted, "It makes sense that emotions get high when Israel is brought up. But for it to come up in a conversation about not hating people for their religion is just destructive." Indeed, often, with Israel and Zionism as the proxy or stand-in topics for deep-seated issues within and outside the Jewish community, determining whose views are within the range of tolerable, either from the Left or the Right, can either require a lot of soul-searching, or simply a knee-jerk reaction.

Matt opined: "All the 'antis' that are out there, we feel like we have permission to hate them when we don't know the 'other.'" When it comes to Israel, being "anti" is often a matter of perspective, particularly for Generation Zers, who at once prioritize tolerance but are also often quick to "cancel" those organizations or individuals whose views are outside of their determined norms. When it comes to Israel, and the Israeli-Palestinian conflict, Jewish Generation Zers are passionate but not always in the ways that the organized Jewish community might have expected.

In 2014, during the conflict between Israel and the Palestinians in the Gaza Strip known as Operation Protective Edge, an organization named IfNowNow was founded. This organization describes itself as being an American Jewish progressive activist group opposing the Israeli occupation of the West Bank and the Gaza Strip. Its membership is largely young Jewish Americans who protest the American government as well as the American Jewish community's support for Israel. These individuals state that their actions against Israel are informed by Jewish values, but this stance has not stopped many in the Jewish community from disassociating with both the philosophy and the tactics of these protestors.

In 2021, Jewish Harvard graduate student Lucas M. Koerner wrote an article in the *Harvard Crimson* calling for his institution to boycott what he described as Israeli apartheid. He referenced the Boycott, Divestment, and Sanctions, or BDS, movement, which is an international movement centered around isolating Israel through economic measures. For years, the BDS movement has operated on college campuses, with resolutions being introduced by student governments demanding that their schools divest from Israel, and advocating, usually unsuccessfully, for Israel to be made a pariah in the global community. This has manifested in everything from Israeli academics being refused visiting scholar positions to performers and musicians removing Israel from their international tours under pressure from protestors. All of this contributes to the overall goal of anti-normalization of Israel in the world.

The BDS movement as a whole regularly crosses the line into antisemitism. It is not only critical of Israeli policies but vocally questions Israel's right to exist; it advocates not for a Palestinian state alongside Israel but for the removal of Israel altogether.[31] Nonetheless, Jewish students like Koerner sometimes end up being advocates against the interests not just of Israel but of themselves as Jews. Koerner wrote, "My great-grandmother did not escape anti-Semitic terror and second-class status so that a Jewish settler-colonial state purporting to speak in her name could establish what leading Israeli human rights organization B'tselem and even Human Rights Watch—otherwise in lockstep with U.S. foreign policy—describe as an apartheid regime."[32]

Jewish supporters of the BDS movement have been disavowed by many leaders in the mainstream Jewish community. Los Angeles-based Rabbi

David Wolpe said, "Those Jews who support BDS, or deny the legitimacy of the State of Israel, have no place at the table. They should not be invited to speak at synagogues and churches, universities and other institutions that respect rational discourse. They should have the same intellectual status as Klansmen: purveyors of hate."[33] Nonetheless, the number of young Jews who support at least some measurement of boycotting Israel is on the rise. In 2020, a poll conducted by the progressive Zionist movement J Street found that almost one-quarter of American Jews under forty support boycotting Israeli products.[34]

While when it comes to Israel, some American Jews may think that they are separate from the actions of a government and nation across the world, the BDS movement has shown the opposite. In 2015, a weeklong music festival in Spain canceled the scheduled appearance of rapper Matisyahu from performing due to pressure, coercion, and threats from the BDS movement.[35] Matisyahu, an American Jew, does not hold Israeli citizenship but still was targeted because he had previously expressed support for Israel. With the majority of Jewish Americans falling into the same category, they inherently are also at risk for falling victim to "cancel culture" for their beliefs on Israel and the legitimacy of Zionism.

The modern State of Israel is the world's first encounter with Jewish autonomy in over two thousand years. It is also the first time that many Jews themselves have had to consider their identities through the lens of power instead of weakness. For Generation Zers, there has never been a world without Israel. Nor has there ever been a true feeling of threat that Israel's very existence may end, leaving Jews vulnerable as a stateless minority once again, as was so internalized in the collective psyche of previous generations. There is a comfort, perhaps false, that comes with the confidence of never having experienced the kind of minority status that comes with not having a proverbial exit strategy.

When I teach my Generation Z–aged students about Israel, I always start by acknowledging biases. For Generation Zers, there is often an initial sense of indignation when confronted with this term, and for fellow educators and communal professionals, there's a discomfort with using it at all. After all, bias is bad—and antisemitism when it relates to Israel often involves accusations of Jews being biased toward Israel and against Palestinians. During May 2021's outbreak of violence between the Israelis and the Palestinians, Jewish communities around the United States organized rallies in solidarity with Israel. When I attended a local solidarity rally, I ran into the parent of a high school senior I had previously worked with, who approached me in a state of distress. "My daughter won't come today. She said that this event is one-sided, and it's not a peace event, and she didn't feel comfortable coming. Will you talk to her and tell her she's wrong?"

I had to respond that I couldn't. Her daughter was not wrong. The event *was* intentionally one sided; it was an event to support Israel. While the ultimate vision was one of peace, it was through the lens of Jewish connections to Israel and Israelis. Bias doesn't have to be a bad thing, but it's critical that it not be glossed over and sugarcoated. Generation Zers are critical thinkers, and they are aware of the world around them. But they often lack context and are likely to jump headlong into a cause célèbre without necessarily having the historical and current affairs backgrounds for a full understanding of the given situation.

My biases when it comes to Israel are complex. Israel is at once a place I fundamentally consider to be my homeland, and yet I've chosen, at least at this moment, to live outside of it. It is the place where I'm able to be the best version of myself. However, as a Jewish educator, I often feel that I make more of a professional impact in my work educating teens in the Diaspora than I did during my years in Israel. I am inherently linked to Israel, through blood, through family, through the innate knowledge that this land and these people are critical to my sense of self as a Jew. And then I ask my students, "What's your Israel story? Whether or not you've been there, whether or not you choose to associate yourself with Israel, as a Jew, there will be those who connect you with Israel, for better or for worse." Therefore, having a sense of what one's Israel story is part of the American Jewish experience.

In May 2021, U.S. Representative Ilhan Omar of Minnesota tweeted, "We must have the same level of accountability and justice for all victims of crimes against humanity. We have seen unthinkable atrocities committed by the U.S., Hamas, Israel, Afghanistan, and the Taliban." This pronouncement sparked outrage at Representative Omar's comparison of both Israel and the United States to recognized terrorist organizations Hamas and the Taliban. However, when responding to the outcry, Representative Omar said with regard to her Jewish colleagues in the House of Representatives, "I welcome at any time my colleagues have asked to have a conversation, to learn from them for them to learn from me. I think it's really important for these members to realize they haven't been partners in—in justice. They haven't been equally engaging in seeking justice around the world and I think I will continue to do that. It is important for me as someone who knows what it feels like to experience injustice in ways that many of my colleagues don't."[36]

By associating her Jewish colleagues with Israel and subsequently accusing them of not being globally justice-minded, Omar fell into the age-old antisemitic trope of insinuating that Jews do not belong in their adopted countries and that their loyalties are questionable. This is a problem on both sides of the political aisle. In 2020, President Donald Trump was also condemned by Jewish organizations for saying to a delegation of American Jewish leaders, "We really appreciate you, we love your country [Israel] also and thank you very much."[37]

Therein lies the paradox. American Jewish educators, leaders, and communal institutions want young American Jews to feel connected with Israel. To feel a link to it that stretches across time and space and makes traveling to Israel a homecoming rather than a moment of tourism. To be prepared to advocate for Israel, and to defend Israel against an ever-growing array of detractors. But at the same time, being told that there is a responsibility to Israel that somehow outweighs one's Americanness is seen as a threat and a source of deep, existential concern.

Rabbi Lord Jonathan Sacks, the late former chief rabbi of the United Kingdom, noted that "at some stage, Jews stopped defining themselves by the reflection they saw in the eyes of God, and started defining themselves by the reflection they saw in the eyes of their Gentile neighbors."[38] When it comes to Jewish Generation Z and Israel, the experience is both internal and external. There is a sense that young Jews have of wanting to be accepted, wanting to be on the right side of history. And anti-Israel sentiments that are directed toward them raise ingrained fears and trauma of what can happen when Jews are accused of disloyalty, injustice, and evil. Being associated with such things, often without the grounding in facts to respond confidently, is a scary and disenchanting reality.

Brad noted, "Bigotry and violence are based on ideas about other people and our relationships to them, and our own relationships in the world." In the span of the seventy-plus years of the existence of the modern State of Israel, the idea of the Jewish people has fundamentally shifted for much of the world. In the early years, when Israel was a fledgling country fighting for its survival against the enormity of the entire Arab world, much of the world cheered. A country seen as being comprised largely of pitiable Holocaust survivors turned into warriors was a source of inspiration and praise for those watching from around the world. But as Israel grew in strength and security, the world that loves an underdog stopped seeing Israel as the fledgling nation it had been and began seeing it, instead, as the aggressor. As sympathies shifted in the ever-evolving Israel–Palestinian conflict, many Jews went from seeing Israel as an unquestionable source of pride to considering it a complicated, sometimes frightening subject.

Israel's position for Generation Zers is unlike that which has been the reality for any previous demographic cohort since the creation of the modern country in 1948. The complexity of Israel is front and center for this generation. Lily, who works with Generation Zers in the Israel engagement space, reflected, "They need a way to reconcile and to understand all the really complex things they're seeing in the world around identity, race, different forms of oppression, and what it means to grapple with them. When they talk about Israel, and what their relationships with Israel are, how do they confront the harder stuff?"

Whereas for previous generations, Israel was a point of unity within the Jewish community and a beacon of unity for non-Jewish allies, for Generation Z, it's often a point of contention. Antisemites on the Left ostracize Israel as a purported violator of human rights, and antisemites on the Right perpetuate a view of Jews as having dual loyalties. In both instances, a shared conflagration of Jews and Israel place American Jews, including Generation Zers, in a position of having to answer for, justify, and explain actions taken by a country that they may not agree with, may never have been to, and may have no context for. By putting young Jews on the defensive when it comes to Israel, a great deal of possibly irreparable damage has been done regarding the relationships that they are able to have with the Jewish state. If loving Israel means defending its actions no matter what, it's no wonder why many Jewish Generation Zers feel distanced from the country. And if by virtue of the threats being made against Israel and the biases Israel faces on college campuses, by political leaders, and in social justice circles, nuanced Israel education is abandoned in favor of advocacy, talking points, and workshops on how to defend it, checking out becomes a more attractive option for young Jews as they come of age.

I fell in love with Israel when I was nine years old. This love was pure because it was on my own terms. No one told me that I had to love Israel or that I had any obligations in this relationship. As such, it could progress purely at my pace—and it rapidly turned into a full-blown love affair. Like the child of a parent who ascribes to the fandom of a particular sports team, no one had to lay things out for me in any kind of explicit way. I was born to love Israel because I'm a Jew, because my ancestors loved it and were kept from it, because it's the one place in the world where being Jewish is a homecoming, no matter where you were born. Like the majority of Jews, including the majority of Generation Zers, I'm a supporter of Israel. I proudly call myself a Zionist—someone who believes in the right of the Jewish people to self-determination in the historic land that we came from.

I also know that Israel is not perfect. As with any true love, I approach Israel with open eyes. I can see its brightest spots and its flaws. Finding out about Israel's faults did not shatter any utopian illusion that I had about Israel, because I knew it intimately—not as a Jewish Disneyland but as a real place that I have an emotional and physical stake in. Part of that is knowing that the story of Israel is not an exclusively Jewish one. The Palestinian people have their own legitimate history, which is not my place to recount here. What I can say, with supreme confidence, is that Generation Z is inheriting an unsustainable reality. With dueling, polarizing spheres of antisemitism, and growing internal divisions, Israel's place in the American Jewish psyche is at a pivot point.

Jewish theologian Abraham Joshua Heschel visited Israel soon after the Six-Day War in 1967 and published his reflections on his experience in 1969 in *Israel: An Echo of Eternity.* In this text, he wrote, "The major weakness was to take the State of Israel for granted, to cease wonder at the marvel of its sheer being. Even the extraordinary tends to be forgotten. Familiarity destroys the sense of surprise. We have been beset by a case of spiritual amnesia. We forgot the daring, the labor, the course of the seers of the State of Israel, of the builders and pioneers."[39] Mara had a similar reflection. "We were taught to be tourists in Israel and to like the food and the music. But actually loving it isn't something we learned."

Being a voice for Israel in the face of rising antisemitism cannot be boiled down to a set of sound bites, however extensive, or a series of ready-to-go facts, however accurate and nuanced. Ultimately, each individual in relationship with Israel is an authentic voice, however that manifests, and finding one's voice in those relationships is part of the mission of the American Jewish experience.

NOTES

1. Braunold, J., & Abuarquob, H. (2015, July 2). A bigger threat than BDS: Anti-normalization. *Haaretz.* Retrieved from https://www.haaretz .com/jewish/.premium-worse-than-bds-anti-normalization-1.5374940

2. The Washington Institute for Near East Policy (2002, October 4). Policy analysis: Implications of a "security fence" for Israel and the

Palestinians. Retrieved from https://www.washingtoninstitute.org/policy-analysis/implications-security-fence-israel-and-palestinians

3. Shavit, A. (2013). *My promised land: The triumph and tragedy of Israel*. New York: Random House.

4. https://zioness.org

5. Jewish Virtual Library (n.d.). A definition of Zionism. Retrieved from jewishvirtuallibrary.org/a-definition-of-zionism

6. Sharansky, N. (2004). 3D test of anti-semitism: Demonization, double standards, delegitimization. *Jewish Political Studies Review.*

7. Rosenthal, H. (2011, December 5). "Remarks at the 2011 B'nai B'rith international policy conference." U.S. Department of State.

8. Dershowitz, A. (2003). *The case for Israel*. Hoboken, NJ: John Wiley & Sons.

9. International Holocaust Remembrance Alliance (2016, May 26). Working definition of antisemitism press release.

10. Cotler, I. (2011, July 7). On judging the distinction between legitimate criticism and demonization. Engage. Retrieved from https://engageonline.wordpress.com/2011/07/07/irwin-cotler-on-judging-the-distinction-between-legitimate-criticism-and-demonization

11. Friedman, T. (2002, October 16). Campus hypocrisy. *New York Times*. Retrieved from https://nytimes.com/2002/10/16/opinion/campus-hypocrisy.htm

12. Magid, J. (2021, March 20). Poll: Americans' support for Israel high; approval for PA and Palestinians rises. *Times of Israel*. Retrieved from https://www.timesofisrael.com/poll-americans-support-for-israel-still-high-approval-for-pa-rises

13. Laitman, M. (2017, July 5). When Chicago Dyke March bans a Jewish Pride flag, Jews should feel unsafe. *Jerusalem Post.*

14. Ziri, D. (2019, June 6). D.C. Dyke March bans Israeli and Jewish symbols on Pride flags, sparking criticism. *Haaretz.*

15. Campbell, A. J. (2019, June 6). The D.C. Dyke March won't let me fly the Jewish Pride flag. Tablet.

16. Gunz, R. (2020, January 21). Campus anti-semitism made me a Zionist. *Jewish Journal*. Retrieved from https://jewishjournal.com/first-person/309725/campus-anti-semitism-made-me-a-zionist

17. Salazar, A. M. (2016, December 21). Organizers hope Women's March on Washington inspires, evolves. NPR.

18. Weiss, B. (2017, July 21). Opinion: When progressives embrace hate. *New York Times.*

19. Kicinich, J. (2018, November 19). A record number of women were just elected, but the Women's March is imploding. Daily Beast.

20. JTA (2018, November 21). Linda Sarsour apologizes to Woman's March Jewish members for slow response to anti-Semitism. *Haaretz.*

21. Meyerson, C. (2017, March 13). Can you be a Zionist feminist? Linda Sarsour says no. *The Nation.* Retrieved from https://www.thenation.com/article/archive/can-you-be-a-zionist-feminist-linda-sarsour-says-no

22. Shire, E. (2020, January 17). How the Women's March made itself irrelevant. *Jewish Telegraphic Agency.* Retrieved from https://www.jta.org/2020/01/17/opinion/how-the-womens-march-made-itself-irrelevant

23. Hersh, E., & Royden, L. (2021, April 9). Antisemitic attitudes across the ideological spectrum. Retrieved from https://www.eitanhersh.com/uploads/7/9/7/5/7975685/hersh_royden_antisemitism_040921.pdf

24. Lipstadt, D. E. 2019. *Antisemitism: Here and now.* New York: Schocken.

25. Pew Research Center. (2018, January). Republicans and Democrats grow even farther apart in views of Israel, Palestinians.

26. Green, E. (2016, August 18). Why do Black activists care about Palestine? *The Atlantic.*

27. Hersh, E., & Royden, L. (2021, April 9). Antisemitic attitudes across the ideological spectrum. Retrieved from https://www.eitanhersh.com/uploads/7/9/7/5/7975685/hersh_royden_antisemitism_040921.pdf

28. Sales, B. (2021, April 22). Conservatives more likely than liberals to hold anti-Semitic views, survey finds. *Jewish Telegraphic Agency.* Retrieved from https://www.jta.org/2021/04/22/united-states/conservatives-are-more-likely-than-liberals-to-hold-anti-semitic-views-survey-finds

29. Gunz, R. (2020, January 21). Campus anti-Semitism. Made Me a Zionist. *Jewish Journal.* Retrieved from https://jewishjournal.com/first-person/309725/campus-anti-semitism-made-me-a-zionist/.

30. *Self-Hating Jews: The legacy of self-hatred.* My Jewish Learning.

31. Jewish News Service (2020, June 2). BDS co-founder says goal of movement is end of Israel. *Israel Hayom.* Retrieved from https://www.israelhayom.com/2020/06/02/bds-co-founder-says-goal-of-movement-is-end-of-israel

32. Koerner, L. M. (2021, June 9). Boycott Israeli apartheid: If not now, when? *Harvard Crimson.* Retrieved from https://www.thecrimson.com/article/2021/6/9/koerner-boycott-israeli-apartheid

33. Goldberg, J. (2011, February 15). How big should the big tent be? *The Atlantic.*

34. Mansoor, S. (2020, December 4). The Trump administration is cracking down against a global movement to boycott Israel. Here's what you need to know about BDS. *Time*. Retrieved from https://time.com/5914975/what-to-know-about-bds

35. A Rototom Sunsplash public institutional declaration regarding Matisyahu.

36. Israel Hayom (2021, July 7). Jewish leaders excoriate Ilhan Omar for latest bigoted rant. Retrieved from https://www.israelhayom.com/2021/07/02/jewish-leaders-excoriate-ilhan-omar-for-latest-bigoted-rant

37. Seddiq, O. (2020, September 17). "Textbook anti-Semitism": American Jews condemn Trump for repeatedly telling them that Israel is "your country." *Business Insider*. Retrieved from https://www.businessinsider.com/american-jews-condemn-trump-for-saying-israel-is-your-country-2020-9

38. Sacks, J. (2009). *Future tense: Jews, Judaism, and Israel in the twenty-first century.* New York: Schocken. p. 59.

39. Heschel, A. J. (1969). *Israel: An echo of eternity.* New York: Farrar, Straus and Giroux.

SIX

Jewish Stars, Shirts, and Swag

As a high school student, I regularly accessorized my outfits with a Jewish star necklace. I could often be found wearing T-shirts with Jewish and Israeli symbols on them, and at one point I ironed a decorative Israeli Defense Forces patch onto my backpack. I was proud of my Judaism, and it became increasingly important for me to display it publicly. As with many identity-defining attributes, I wanted my outsides to match my insides. I cared so much about being Jewish, and it felt compelling to literally wear my feelings. While to me this always made sense, I soon came to realize that it wasn't necessarily simple. Wearing insignia identifying oneself as Jewish is a complex and multifaceted phenomenon that speaks to generational privilege and an ability to claim this identity without fear of retribution, and it can be a source of contention for many. For every impassioned think piece about why we should wear our stars proudly and walk through the world without fear,[1] there's an equally compelling counterpoint that speaks to legitimate concerns about personal safety that are assuaged by taking this one step to cover up in order to blend in and assimilate.[2]

In my case, the debate over my star came to a head when I was traveling to Europe with a friend. In celebration of our high school graduation, we planned to spend three weeks split between France and Greece. As anyone would have been, I was incredibly excited about the trip. I bought new clothes and a backpack to fit the look, and I put together the perfect travel packing list. And then my grandmother came over and started yelling at me. She was appalled that I had no intention of removing my silver Jewish star necklace, that I had included T-shirts emblazoned with Hebrew writing in my travel wardrobe, and that I had every intention of traveling while proudly presenting my Judaism to anyone who saw me. She was proud of my pride, but as a product of the Holocaust, she was afraid of me walking around in what she saw as potentially hostile environments with a target literally on my body.

My grandmother wasn't alone in her worries about presenting as Jewish, in the United States, and particularly abroad. European antisemitism has been known to be on the rise and to manifest in a more violent fashion than its North American counterpart does. According to a 2018 poll from the European Agency for Fundamental Human Rights, 40 percent of Europe's Jews have considered leaving their home countries.[3] Too often, the need to consider this measure comes from a place of real, visceral fears. In 2017, Sarah Falimi, a French doctor, teacher, and Orthodox Jew was killed in her apartment in Paris and thrown out the window of the third-floor residence.[4] Her assailant, Kobili Traoré, shouted "Allahu Akbar"[5] after pushing Sarah, who was the only Jewish resident of her building. Afterward, he said that he had killed "the Satan," but it took months for French courts, and much of the media, to name the murder as an act of antisemitism.[6] Compounding this, in April 2021, four years after the murder, France's highest court affirmed the decision of the lower courts: Traoré would not be tried, having been deemed not responsible for his actions due to being on drugs at the time of the attack.[7]

In reaction to the verdict, the president of the Representative Council of Jewish Institutions in France, Francis Kalifat, delivered the chilling words: "From now on in our country, we can torture and kill Jews with complete impunity."[8] With the increase in attacks on and murders of visibly Jewish individuals and the new resignation to what is seen as a lack of strong-enough consequences, it is not surprising that French Jews and their counterparts elsewhere around the world in general and in Europe in particular are seeking exit avenues and making strategic decisions with regard to what it means to present as Jewish to the public.

Addison is a Jewish mother of two, and a military spouse. As such, her family has had the relatively unique experience of living in different communities around the world, including a stint in Italy. When her older child was born, she wanted to give him a Jewish first name, and her husband objected. However, by the time their younger child was born, his opinions had changed, and he was open to a visibly Jewish name. But by that point, Addison didn't want to have one child with a Jewish name and not the other, so they made the intentional, conscious decision to give general, secular names. They have built Jewish lives and circles, both inside and outside of their home, in each location. However, as Addison reflects on their time in Europe in particular, she remembers a difference. "We would visit old synagogues and Jewish quarters all over Europe. I would always be on alert, looking around in a different way, when we were in those kinds of places." Addison notes that in the United States, as well as in Europe, synagogue security has become normalized. While she would not change her family's routines and practices at this point, she emphasizes the increased sense of awareness that follows her. "My son has an IDF T-shirt. I wouldn't tell him not to wear it in public, but I would definitely be more aware of our surroundings and the situation we're in if he did."

Rob, the high school sophomore from Texas who has been involved in Holocaust education, described the intentionality behind his decision to wear a certain Jewish symbol. He decided to wear a *chai* necklace, a symbol of Hebrew letters representing the word meaning "life."[9] By opting for this symbol instead of the better-known and more easily recognized Star of David, Rachel sought to use her sartorial choices to start conversations. "I got the *chai* because it's a way to show my faith to others. People who aren't curious won't ask. But because it's not a Star of David and everyone doesn't know what it is, if they're curious enough and they do ask, there's room for us to have a conversation."

"I remember when I was younger, I was out shopping with my mom and I told her that I wanted something for Chanukah. She shushed me, and I didn't understand why. But now that I'm older, I get it. I don't talk loudly about being Jewish in public anymore." Arielle, the Instagram content creator from Connecticut, recounted this story to demonstrate what it means for her to present Jewishly in public. She's aware of the ability that she has to "pass" as part of the white majority, and the white privilege she has as a virtue of her skin color, while maintaining her Jewish identity. While being taught not to loudly proclaim her Judaism in public is not in and of itself an expression of antisemitism, the reluctance to affiliate with this identifier in unknown settings is demonstrative of how pervasive the culture of antisemitism is.

"After the shooting [at Congregation Tree of Life in Pittsburgh] I started wearing my kippah[10] more in public. I take the metro to school every day, and I wear my kippah. Sometimes I run into other Jewish people, and it's fun to have a connection. But I definitely understand people who are scared of something happening when you look Jewish in public. For me, I feel like it's better to show that we're here, we're not going anywhere, we're still Jewish, and we're going to stay Jewish. There's not anything anyone's going to do about it." Zeke, the Marylander whom we met earlier, views presenting as Jewish externally as an internal manifestation of his feelings of Jewish pride and connection. For him, it's simple to physically claim his Judaism. But for others, the choice can be far more fraught.

Amanda Berman, the Zioness founder and executive director, relayed a story of why it's so important for Zioness leaders and activists to show up with signs, shirts, and other visible insignia identifying them as Zionists. At the Women's March in Los Angeles in 2018, a contingent of Zioness leaders marched, bedecked in their Zioness shirts, holding signs and flags showcasing their cause and allegiances. There they encountered a mother and daughter. The daughter, then eleven years old, wore a green sweatshirt. The mother explained that the shirt was actually an Israel Defense Forces sweatshirt, but that fellow marchers had yelled at her daughter and told her that she could not participate in the March while wearing it. They so intimidated the preteen that she turned her shirt inside out so as to avoid further harassment. But seeing Zioness allies proudly displaying their own paraphernalia inspired her, showing her that she wasn't alone and could simultaneously be a supporter of Israel and of progressive feminism in the United States. This demonstration of external Jewish pride gave a sense of safety and security to someone whose equilibrium had been badly shaken in that moment. But as Generation Zers continue to make their own sartorial choices, would this particular one make the same choice again? Or will the memory of her antagonists, in what was supposed to have been a supportive environment, keep her sweatshirt on inside out?

Elisheva, the Jewish/Romani Instagrammer, came down on the side of caution when it comes to presenting as Jewish in public. "A lot of Jews don't feel safe wearing their Stars of David. There's a feeling of having to hide your Jewishness. It's not the same as skin color, because you can take it off, but it's a really hurtful reality to have to consider it." For her, the COVID-19 pandemic and accompanying social distancing measures have provided some relief from the anxiety she experiences when navigating her Jewish identity in public. "I'm scared. But since COVID, I feel like I have the excuse and I can feel less guilty about not wanting to leave my house and watching services on Zoom than figuring out my safety and doing it in person."

Melinda, the mother of a Generation Zer in the Washington, DC, area, shared the generational differences between herself and her daughter when it comes to presenting Jewishly in public. "My daughter wears Jewish shirts out of pride, rather than defiance, whereas I totally do the defiant thing. When I was in graduate school in Chicago, I lived near the home of Louis Farrakhan, and I used to intentionally jog past his house wearing Hebrew shirts as an 'F you' kind of thing. But I hope that's not something I've passed down. I like that my daughter's Jewish pride is unencumbered."

Kathy also recognizes the generational differences when it comes to presenting Jewishly. She is a Brooklyn native who lives in the Midwest. When she grew up in New York, there was a physical reality of antisemitism that her Generation Z children have never experienced. "They don't have the same burden of antisemitism that I perceived growing up." In that regard, she remembers an incident when she was in a store with her then-young child, who announced "Mommy, I know what I want for Chanukah!" A fellow patron of the store turned around and said, "Huh, that kid doesn't have a Jewish nose. I wouldn't have guessed she'd want a Chanukah gift." Kathy reminisced, "And then my kid looked at her and said, 'I'm Jewish and this is my nose, so that must be what a Jewish nose looks like.' It didn't fase her at all." For many parents, raising proud Jewish Generation Zers means, among other things, creating a comfort with Judaism that enables them to move through the world without the burden of the specter of antisemitism. Sociologists Robert Fine and Philip Spencer are thinkers who have put the onus of antisemitism onto the non-Jewish world, rather than on Jews, to figure out how to counter. Antisemitism, from their perspective, is a construct of the non-Jewish imagination that's projected onto Jews.[11]

Shira is a mother of five and identifies as an Orthodox Jew. But she's not particularly focused on Jewish identity. "I think about Jewish learning, Jewish knowledge, Jewish fluency and literacy much more than Jewish identity. I think that comes along with all of the rest of those things." Shira's husband is a clergy member, and as such, their family is very Jewishly visible in the communities that they spend time in. There's an increasing sense of awareness of what it means to be recognizable as Jews. This isn't always necessarily a bad thing. Once, when a group of students who had been invited to Shabbat dinner got lost on the way to the home of the host, they stopped someone on the street to ask for directions. The person immediately said, "Oh, you're looking for the rabbi's house! I know which one that is." While this was not an experience of antisemitism, Shira noted, "There's an awareness that everyone knows who we are. When we socialize outside, something we did much more during the pandemic, people saw: the Jewish family lives there. The rabbi's family lives there." As has previously been noted, Jews who look visibly, largely meaning stereotypically, Jewish, are at a greater risk for antisemitic attacks than their counterparts. In July 2021, a rabbi from the Chabad Lubavitch movement, Rabbi Shlomo Noginski, was stabbed multiple times in Boston, Massachusetts. As part of the outcry that followed, local Jewish organizations issued a statement: "As a community, an attack on one of us is an attack on all of us. If one of us feels vulnerable, we are all vulnerable. We will not be silent, and we will be there together."[12]

Choosing if and how to present Jewishly in public often involves making decisions about code switching. Code switching is a behavioral adjustment that involves adjusting one's style of speech, appearance, behavior, and expression in ways that will optimize the comfort of others in exchange for fair treatment, quality service, and employment opportunities.[13] It has long been used by Black people attempting to successfully navigate interracial interactions and can be either a conscious or unconscious decision. Code switching is often engaged in for a variety of reasons, from wanting to fit in to wanting to ingratiate oneself to others to wanting to convey thoughts publicly but while still maintaining a degree of circumspect secrecy.[14]

For Jewish Americans, code switching often happens when they are questioning whether or not they're in a safe space to express their Judaism. A University of Indiana freshman I spoke with shared the choices that he made when meeting new people on campus. "When people ask what I did the year between high school and college, I usually just say I was on a gap year. If I know they're Jewish, or I know them really well and think they'll be cool about it, I'll actually say I was in Israel."

Brad, whose work focuses on antisemitism on a national scale, noted that as minorities, Jews in the United States can feel like they lack representation, despite the abundance of Jews in certain industries. "No matter how powerful a position you occupy, you're still under all of these pressures and it feels like you can only be yourself within certain parameters. Even when we achieve some degree of representation and visibility, there are still all kinds of ways where that is circumscribed." For many Generation Zers, key elements of their Jewish identities are put into Americanized terms in order to fit in, are thereby code switched from uniquely Jewish and therefore particularistic into universalist means of expression. Nowhere is this more prevalent than in the language used around social justice inside and outside of Jewish communal spaces.

Tikkun olam is a phrase most commonly heard as a slogan for activism, political involvement, and social justice. It has become a catchall in many ways, coming to stand in for almost any laudable value, including energy conservation, recycling, government health care packages, the fight against terrorism, better nutrition, looking after stray animals, and so on.[15] As tikkun olam has assimilated into modern, liberal discourse, it has both inspired and connected Jews and become a source of contention, as its overuse has, for many, diluted the intended meaning of the phrase.

Hillary Clinton used the phrase "tikkun olam" in a 2019 speech to the Jewish Labor Committee. Then–vice president elect Kamala Harris spoke about tikkun olam in her 2020 Chanukah address, with Jewish husband Doug Emhoff. "It [Chanukah] is a celebration of tikkun olam, which is about fighting for justice and fighting for the dignity of all people."[16] Democratic presidential hopeful, Jewish billionaire Michael Bloomberg tweeted that his political mission stemmed from tikkun olam. "My parents taught me that Judaism is about more than going to shul—it's about living our values to help others and to 'repair the world' in the tradition of Tikkun Olam. That's the spirit behind our campaign, and it's why I'm excited to launch our new coalition #UnitedforMike."[17]

Like their millennial Jewish counterparts, Generation Zers increasingly identify with tikkun olam as a means of expressing their Judaism. Lia, a high school senior in Virginia, shared, "My Judaism makes me look at the world with more compassion and empathy than I would otherwise. When you hear about religious discrimination, or any form of discrimination, Judaism reminds me that my people have fought for a chance, for equality, and to be accepted. It reminds me that I can't just say this isn't my problem and move on." Further, in a reflection on the appeal of tikkun olam as a core tenet of Jewish identity, Maytal Kuperard shared, "We *do* "Peoplehood" when we commit to universal justice, voluntary service, and acts of *chesed* [lovingkindness] whether inside or outside of our community. It's how we locate ourselves within the minority amongst other minorities. It's that particular feeling we are greeted with when acknowledging the part the Jewish community is playing in seeking to provide refuge for unaccompanied Syrian minors in London today."[18]

It is understood that young Jews identify with the call to social action that they see in tikkun olam and how it connects the particularism of their Judaism to the universalist causes they espouse, on both sides of the political aisle. But the decision whether to call it tikkun olam or to use the universalist, American phrases of "social action" and "social justice" is often made depending upon the circumstances and the codes that they call for. "My Judaism is what brings me to the progressive spaces that I spend time in. But I usually don't say that, because I don't want to start a conversation about how I feel about Israel. Bringing up being Jewish runs the risk of making everything awkward." A University of Michigan sophomore, who is involved with feminist, LGBTQ, and environmental progressive causes, knows what drives her. But she only uses the language of tikkun olam to describe her social activism in certain self-determined safe spaces.

Brad noted that "a rose is no less a flower because it has its own particular beauty. It's not taking away from the universal beauty of flowers for one to have a unique presentation." While the trend in the United States, and in many places around the world, is toward universalism and away from particularist mentalities,[19] using uniquely Jewish language and wearing Jewish-associated clothing allows young Jews to self-identify and to intentionally claim what connects them and sets them apart from the anonymous collective. Elana, a high school student in Maryland, reflected, "Most people are white, Christian, and they may not understand what it's like to be discriminated against in any way. I feel like being Jewish adds so much—community, sympathy, and just calling me to be a better person." Scott, a high school senior from New York, noted that being part of a minority group is what connects him with his Jewish identity. "I feel the most Jewish when I'm around non-Jewish people. Sometimes when people are talking about their families or cultural upbringing, like food, or just family relationships, I'll realize that there are tendencies that I have that are associated with being Jewish, and I feel like I'm part of something different."

As American Jews make the choice whether to claim their Judaism in non-Jewish spaces, the reasons for not doing so can range from concerns about physical safety to emotional well-being to wanting to be accepted by the diverse groups that they spend time with. It is known that those who present as visibly Jewish are at a higher risk of antisemitic attacks and vitriol,[20] so the reason why, for many, there is a choice to be made about their Judaism can be easily understood. A Boston-based college freshman whom I spoke with reminisced about his first encounters with antisemitism. "My brothers and I went to Jewish day schools our whole lives. We always wore our kippot, even when we played basketball. Our school was in a league for religious private schools, but since we were the only Jewish ones, we played against Catholic and Christian schools in the Boston area. When we would have away games, there would be antisemitic slurs and comments about Jews, from the other team and from their families in the stands."

Sometimes, when "looking Jewish" is someone's lived experience, when they're treated differently, it's not always clear what the motivation is. Idan, whose father is the president of their synagogue, reflected on the experience of transitioning from synagogue services to backyard Shabbat experiences during the COVID-19 pandemic. "There was one day when we had to walk the Torah from the yard back to the synagogue. We live in this super quiet suburban development. My dad and I were walking in the street to bring the Torah back to the synagogue, and all of a sudden, this guy was driving behind us and honking that we should get off the street. They said we had no business being there. I have no reason to think that wasn't antisemitic, but I'm not sure. They could have just meant walking in the street. But at the same time, we both had a kippah on, and I'm assuming that's why it happened."

In June 2021, a meme circulated on social media from @Antoniogm (Antonio García Martínez):

1: Let's drop all the public Jewy stuff and support for Israel, it's dangerous out there now

2: I WANT A MAGEN DAVID THE SIZE OF A DINNER PLATE AROUND MY NECK

When it comes to presenting Jewishly in public, every choice that each individual makes feels deeply personal and legitimate. If individuals are frightened for their safety when they claim their Judaism in physical ways, or if they don't want to be on display as representatives of the Jewish community and opt to fly under the radar, this is not indicative of Jewish shame. Rather than being a commentary on an individual, it's an indictment of the society that person lives in that makes it feel like being a Jew is something that needs to be somehow private. Likewise, for those who choose to present loudly and proudly, this can be a beautiful thing, particularly when it's done for the right reasons. To show one's pride is great, when it's on your own terms. But for someone's Judaism to manifest purely as a statement of defiance to detractors is its own potentially fraught reality.

"Judaism should be a joyous experience. Antisemitism isn't, and shouldn't be, our major raison d'être when it comes to being Jewish. We take it seriously, of course. But if it becomes what defines our Jewish identity, they win." Lily, who works with Jewish teens, summed things up succinctly. Pride is encouraged and championed, always. But a Judaism based on defiance is not sustainable, and it is certainly not transferable. If Generation Zers respond to antisemitism by focusing all of their efforts on countering hatred and detractors, they may find real meaning in their activism and self-advocacy. But they run the very real risk of losing sight of the why behind the what. Any identity that is based on what it runs counter to, rather than the value that it brings, lacks sufficient grounding. So when Jewish sartorial choices are made, whether they are for religious observance or cultural adherence, their value to the wearer comes from how they experience embodied Judaism, not in how others react to their choices.

One Generation Zer reflected on their practice of volunteering in their community every year on Christmas Day. "I don't usually wear a kippah, but I always do on Christmas. I want people to know that Jews are doing things that they might not think of us as doing. This is how I make sure that people know, when I go out into the world, that I'm a Jew, and this is what a Jew looks like."

As for me, what it means to dress and look Jewishly is a complex set of norms. My naturally frizzy brown hair and asymmetrical nose are straight out of a stereotype of what Eastern European Judaism is. Those aspects of my being were not my choice, but they are realities I have come to love and appreciate. What is my choice is the Jewish star that I wear around my neck, one that I picked out myself as a child on a trip to Israel. And the themed Jewish leggings and T-shirts I wear for each holiday embody who I am as a Jewish educator. I'm proud. I find the joy. And while perhaps what's inside should be enough, I want others to know it. It's important to me that members of my community, as well as random passersby in the public sphere, know who I am, and particularly that fellow Jews who may be hesitant to show off realize that they aren't alone.

NOTES

1. Dizik, A. (2015, August 18). Let freedom bling. *Tablet*. Retrieved from https://www.tabletmag.com/sections/community/articles/let-freedom-bling

2. Woolfson, L. (2020, February 19). Why I stopped wearing a Jewish star. *Washington Jewish Week*. Retrieved from https://www.washingtonjewishweek.com/64341/why-i-stopped-wearing-a-jewish-star/editorial-opinion

3. Buck, T. (2018, December 10). Anti-semitism prompts 40% of European Jews to consider emigration. *Financial Times*. Retrieved from https://www.ft.com/content/a8f26a56-fc62-11e8-aebf-99e208d3e521

4. Theise, P. (2020, May 1). Hundreds rally in Paris to seek justice for murdered Jewish woman Sarah Halimi. France24.

5. "God is great," in Arabic.

6. Berman, L. (2021, April 23). Sister of murdered French Jewish woman Sarah Halimi to ask Israel to try case. *Times of Israel.* Retrieved from https://www.timesofisrael.com/sister-of-murdered-french-jewish-woman-sarah-halimi-to-ask-israel-to-try-case

7. France24 (2021, April 14). Top French court upholds decision not to try suspect in Jewish woman's murder. Retrieved from https://www.france24.com/en/france/20210414-top-french-court-upholds-decision-not-to-try-suspect-in-jewish-woman-s-murder

8. Collins, L. (2021, April 22). My word: Justice for Sarah Halimi and justice for all. *Jerusalem Post.* Retrieved from https://www.jpost.com/opinion/my-word-justice-for-sarah-halimi-and-justice-for-all-666062

9. Philologos (2012, November 11). Exploring "chai" culture. *Jewish Daily Forward.* Retrieved from https://forward.com/culture/165445/exploring-chai-culture/?p=all

10. Skullcap.

11. Fine, R., & Spencer, P. (2017). *Antisemitism and the Left: On the return of the Jewish question.* Manchester, UK: Manchester University Press.

12. Sobey, R. (2021, July 1) Boston man faces arraignment today in stabbing of rabbi in Brighton. *Boston Herald.* Retrieved from https://www.bostonherald.com/2021/07/01/rabbi-reportedly-stabbed-outside-jewish-building-in-boston

13. McCluney, C. L., Robotham, K., Lee, S., Smith, R., & Durkee, M. (2019, November 15). The costs of code switching. *Harvard Business Review.* Retrieved from https://hbr.org/2019/11/the-costs-of-codeswitching

14. Thompson, M. (2013, April 13). Five reasons why people code-switch. NPR. Retrieved from https://www.npr.org/sections/codeswitch/2013/04/13/177126294/five-reasons-why-people-code-switch

15. Cooper, L. (2013). The assimilation of tikkun olam. *Jewish Political Studies Review, 25*(3-4), 2013, pp. 10–42.

16. Hanau, S. (2020, December 11). Trump, Biden, and Harris's Jewish husband wish American Jews a happy Hanukkah. *Times of Israel.* Retrieved from https://www.timesofisrael.com/trump-biden-and-harris-jewish-husband-wish-american-jews-a-happy-hanukkah

17. Bloomberg, M. [@MikeBloomberg] (2020, January 26). "My parents taught me." Twitter.

18. Kuperard, M. (2016, June 19). Peoplehood: Millennials and tikkun olam. *eJewishPhilanthropy*. Retrieved from https://ejewishphilanthropy.com/peoplehood-millennials-and-tikkun-olam

19. Tompkins, D., Galbraith, D., & Tompkins, P. (2010). Universalism, particularism and cultural self-awareness: A comparison of American and Turkish university students. *Journal of International Business and Cultural Studies*. Retrieved from https://www.aabri.com/manuscripts/09324.pdf

20. Pomrenze, Y., & Carroll, J. (2019, September 19). Orthodox Jews fear being targets of rising anti-semitism. CNN. Retrieved from https://www.cnn.com/2019/09/19/us/new-york-orthodox-jews-fear/index.html

SEVEN

But You Don't *Look* Jewish: Diversity within the Jewish Community

The stereotype of a Jewish person in the United States, in many ways, has not changed in generations. For many, the image that comes to mind of a Jewish person is an Ashkenazi Jew[1] with dark, often curly, hair,[2] who is likely wealthy and dwells in a major coastal city.[3] And of course, the ubiquitous Jewish nose,[4] a prominent feature in antisemitic caricatures, abounds. While this has never been an accurate portrayal of Jews, in 2021, the image of Jews as one monolithic-appearing group discounts the facts on the ground. It has been underreported in the recent past,[5] but an increasing number of American Jews self-identify as Jews of color, with a 2020 nationwide study identifying 8 percent of American Jews overall as Black, Hispanic, Asian, or multiracial.[6] That number, however, nearly doubles in the under-thirty demographic, with 15 percent of this population identifying as Jews of color.[7]

Often, antisemitism does not take into account the intersectional identities that are increasingly prevalent in the Jewish community. And for Jews of diverse backgrounds, exploring how their multiple identities inform their choices and actions is a complex process. Alina, a mother of two Generation Zers whose husband does not identify as Jewish, noted her dislike of the often-used phrase "half Jewish." "They are Jewish. They might also be something else, but they're Jewish, and I want them to feel like this is their people and they don't have to apologize for any of that."

Elisheva, the Jewish/Romani Instagrammer we met earlier, grew up knowing that her father wasn't white. "People would ask me why he was brown, and I would say I didn't know. It was only when I was eighteen and I was doing genealogical research that I reconnected with my dad's extended family, and I found out that my ancestors are Sinti and Romani. They lived in a racist area, and they felt safer actually saying that they were Native American than dealing with the stigma of being Romani." While Elisheva's father does not present as white and she has inherited the cultural awareness of being part of a minority within a minority, she is at the same time aware of her white privilege. "I acknowledge that I am seen as a white person in society. I have the privilege of having white skin, and I benefit from the racist system that we're all in."

Sophie, the Chicago native who moved to Phoenix, has self-described as nonconfrontational. When she has encountered antisemitic sentiments, she has described the inner dilemma that accompanies them. "I always have to choose, Do I want to take up the fight and risk losing a friend, or should I just stay quiet and let them get away with it?" She has encountered physical manifestations of antisemitism, and the questions that come with them. "I saw a swastika painted on the sidewalk. It wasn't directed towards me personally, but it was definitely me seeing antisemitism." Her Jewish self-presentation, in addition to bringing up questions of how she clothes herself, has also called up questions about other ways that people carry themselves Jewishly. "People have asked me how I could be in the free lunch program and be Jewish . . . classism in the Jewish community is a huge problem." Indeed, when there's the perception that Jews are a certain way, look a certain way, and act a certain way, it often leads to antisemitic sentiment.

Brad, from his vantage point monitoring antisemitism nationwide, noted, "A lot of antisemitism is based in ignorance. People fill the void of what they don't understand about others with anxieties, fears, and prejudices. So if you can, fill the void preemptively about who Jewish people are, crucially our diversity, because when you homogenize a diverse group of people, you're already stereotyping."

In recent years, the previously unexplored diversity of the American Jewish community has been highlighted, often in unexpected ways. A repeatedly referenced example of nonstereotypical faces of Judaism becoming mainstream is that of Tiffany Haddish's Black Mitzvah. The Grammy-winning comedy special on Netflix highlights Haddish, a Black Jewish comedian, and her celebration of the traditional coming-of-age rite, in a nontraditional way. In honor of her fortieth birthday, Haddish gathered celebrity friends, read from the Torah, and taught the wisdom she had learned along the way of her Jewish journey.[8]

Haddish, who celebrated her Black Mitzvah in December 2019, described the impetus for the public showcasing of her Jewish identity:

> When I came up with the concept for my special, I was trying to figure out a way to tell my truth, my experiences in life, and also maybe open other people's eyes to the fact that in African American culture, there is nothing that says, "Okay, you're officially a woman," or "You're officially a man." There's no ceremony. There's no rite of passage. I remember having this debate with my friends about this. One of my homeboys said, "You know, I've been to jail like three times, I'm a man." Going to jail—I don't think that makes you a man. Knowing who you are, knowing where you come from, *that's* what makes you an adult. And being able to share your story. That's what I love about Judaism, because it's all about sharing your stories and questioning and learning from each other.[9]

Black Mitzvah, and the enthusiastic, overwhelmingly positive feedback it received both inside and outside of the Jewish community, demonstrates that Jews of color are increasingly welcomed and celebrated as authentic faces of Judaism, despite overwhelming stereotypes of Jews looking a certain way, behaving a certain way, and being from certain places. Of course, in many ways, this is only the beginning. The organized Jewish community has a great deal of work to do on creating spaces that are inclusive of both the breadth and depth of members of said communities, on elevating Jews of color into leadership roles, and on unpacking and acknowledging the ways that the experiences of Jews of color are uniquely challenging. Providing platforms, safe and inclusive spaces, and cocreating a reality that is intentionally diverse within the Jewish community is a collective task and is one that Generation Z is ready to meet head-on.

For generations, a key stereotype about Jewish girls in particular was embodied in a special rite of passage: nose jobs. The Jewish nose is an oft-cited antisemitic trope, with political cartoons, jokes, and other visual representations of Jews emphasizing large, prominent noses. The nose job often embodied attempts by Jews to shake off their minority status and to fit in with the larger society. In many ways, the nose job is demonstrative of internalized antisemitism. Rarely would anyone admit that their goal in undergoing rhinoplasty surgery was to look "less Jewish." Instead, their rationales would run toward the generic. "I want to look pretty"; "I want to feel confident." Whether consciously or subconsciously, though, in these statements there is a sense that one's natural, Jewish-associated physical presentation was not enough to correlate with societal expectations of beauty.

Between 2000 and 2011, the American Society of Plastic Surgeons reported a drop of 37 percent in the number of nose jobs performed, among the sharpest in all procedures. While the religion of cosmetic surgery patients is not documented, there is evidence that in the same time period, rhinoplasty grew in popularity among Hispanic and Asian Americans. If the total number of nose jobs in America is rapidly declining while growing in certain demographic group, one potential conclusion is that rhinoplasty is becoming less popular among Jews.[10]

Melvin Konner, the author of *The Jewish Body,* said of the decline in nose jobs, "I think it's because of increased ethnic pride and a decreased desire to stop looking Jewish and blend in . . . which is why rhinoplasty was invented."[11] As the ideal of beauty has changed, and the image of what Jewish looks like has likewise evolved, more and more Jewish adolescents have learned to embrace their inherited features. By 2018, it was reported that nose jobs had fallen 43 percent from 2000.[12] But in 2020, the trend somehow reverted, with an uptick in nose jobs that left the averages at only 9 percent under those of 2000.

So what has changed to make the pendulum swing the other way, and what does it say about Jewish identity? For many Generation Zers, the TikTok trend of #nosejob, which boasts over 2.6 billion views,[13] and "surgery transformation videos" is thought to be a factor. Major TikTok stars, including many Jewish users, have revealed their rhinoplasties. It has been hypothesized that the rise of wellness culture and body positivity have, ironically, served to encourage teens toward elective surgeries. The pervading sense is that if they choose it, the TikTok-ers have the right to do whatever they want with their bodies and can and should take the measures to feel confident as a boon to their mental health.

In an op-ed for the *Jerusalem Post,* Joanna Mann reflected on the psychological damage that the TikTok trends may be having on Jewish Generation Zers. "While we wear this feature [the nose] as a badge of honor today, for me it hasn't always been that way. As a teenager I would straighten my frizzy, wavy hair before school, shave my forearm, and God knows, avoid showing my side profile at all costs. I told myself I would get a nose job before college. Maybe then I would finally be pretty enough to escape the teasing comments and wear a ponytail with pride."[14] While Mann, a Generation Zer herself, no longer feels called to go under the knife in order to feel confident and proud, there are many out there who do not have the same sense of self. As recently as the 2020 Georgia senatorial race, Jewish candidate Jon Ossoff was targeted by his incumbent rival with a campaign ad that enlarged his nose. While the rival, Senator David Perdue, contended that the facial distortion was an unintentional error, many were not convinced of the innocence of the advertisement.[15]

At once, we are in a space where what it means to "look Jewish" is less defined than ever before, but still the stereotypes prevail and remain tools of antisemites to use against Jews. This is problematic both when it comes to interactions with non-Jews and within the ever-broadening borders of the Jewish community itself. As what it means to look Jewish takes on different meanings outside of the vision of a white, curly-haired, big-nosed individual, the Jewish community is grappling with its own assumptions of who is presumed to be Jewish. Security guards at synagogues and other Jewish venues have been asked to start searching the bags of all visitors, for example, in order to avoid racial profiling.[16]

Many synagogues and Jewish communal institutions, both in the United States and around the world, have taken increasingly strict security measures in order to protect the safety of their communities over the years. Since the series of attacks on Jews and Jewish spaces between 2018 and 2020—including the Tree of Life massacre in Pittsburgh; the shooting at a synagogue in Poway, California; a shooting in a kosher grocery store in Jersey City, New Jersey; and the machete attack on a rabbi in his home during his family's celebration of the Chanukah holiday,[17] this feeling of needing security has only grown. As a result, an increasing number of Jewish communal institutions and individuals are feeling the need to include armed guards as part of their security measures. However, many Jews of color are concerned that they will not only have to contend with antisemitism but also discrimination within the Jewish communities that they're a part of.

In a 2018 article, Nylah Burton wrote an article titled, "As a Black Jew, I'm Begging You: Don't Arm Your Synagogue."[18] In it, she highlighted some of the concerns that Jews of color have when it comes to presenting as both nonwhite and Jewish when it comes to their physical safety.

> Black Jews and other Jews of Color are already made to feel as though they don't belong, as though they aren't part of the communities that they've been born or acculturated into. They are already forced to face an incessant barrage of invasive questions about their observance, parentage, and identity when they walk into synagogues.

In the article, Burton profiled Kai, a black Jew from Pennsylvania:

> Kai told me that if the members of their synagogue were armed, they
> would feel the need to attend almost all synagogue events so as not to
> appear "new" or "unfamiliar." Kai said that, "If I miss one Shabbat,
> I might get shot [at] the next [one] by some new idiot."

There is consensus in the face of antisemitism and the phenomenon of
mass shootings in general that the Jewish community's security needs are
legitimate and in need of thorough and careful addressing. However, there
is also a growing movement to ensure that protecting the broader Jewish
community against antisemitism does not involve measures that fail to
account for the needs of Jews of color.

In a 2020 article in the *New York Jewish Week,* former Obama administration liaison to the Jewish community Matt Nosanchuk said that security
"can't come at the expense of black Jews or other black people. . . . We
need to take a hard look at these relationships and . . . if we are partnering
with law enforcement organizations, we need to make sure that they are
observing policies and practices and training that does not turn them into
an agent of systemic racism in our country."[19]

During the ritual of the Passover seder, one of the most well-known
vignettes is that of the four sons, or, in modern, egalitarian versions, the
four children. Each of the four children is an archetype: the Wise Child,
the Wicked Child, the Simple Child, and the Child Who Does Not Know
How to Ask.[20] There are numerous explanations for what each of the four
is meant to represent and how they fit into the Jewish community. The
most obviously controversial is the Wicked Child, who the Haggadah
[Passover prayer book] says asks, "What does this mean to *you*?" The text
then admonishes them for holding themselves separate from the community and for not seeing themselves as part of the collective story of the
exodus from Egypt.[21] By viewing themselves as external and "other," this
child becomes "wicked" and cut off as a result.

In an ever-diversifying United States, what it means to be part of any
given community comes as a result of either an explicit or an implicit
agreement between the individual and the collective. The question of how
the Jewish community intersects and blurs racial and ethnic lines within
the United States is a challenging one, both from within and outside of the
Jewish people. Whether someone feels like they fit in Jewishly can often
be a function of many realities, including their own experiences, their
family's comfort within Jewish communal spaces, and the extent to which
they feel accepted by the collective. To feel othered, particularly when it

comes to the question of race in the Jewish community, is no longer seen as a commentary on the individual. They have not chosen to set themselves apart but instead, too often, have been made to feel "other" by Jews and non-Jews alike.

Unlike in the previous chapter, which focused on the choices that Generation Zers make as they pertain to presenting as Jewish, the intersections between Jewish and racial identity are impermeable and are increasingly complex as the Jewish community continues to diversify. Of course, this is not exclusively a twenty-first-century reality. In a 1993 edition of *The Village Voice,* Michael Lerner wrote,

> In the context of American politics, to be "white" means to be a beneficiary of the past 500 years of European exploration and exploitation of the rest of the world - and hence to "owe" something to those who have been exploited. So when Jews are treated as white in the United States, the assessment is not a crude physical one but a judgment of Jewish culture and civilization, history and destiny. But Jews can only be deemed "white" if there is a massive amnesia on the part of non-Jews about the monumental history of anti-Semitism (which continues to play an important role in European politics today even after Europeans did their best to murder us all off), combined with the willfull accommodation of Jews who have unconsciously internalized the anti-Semitic demands of the larger culture.[22]

Linda, the mother of three Generation Zers, noted, "I don't think a lot of white families feel equipped to talk about race right now, so it's a lot harder to have those conversations in a Jewish context." The very question of whiteness for Jews, as we've seen, is a fraught one. Many Jews shy away from identifying with the white majority in the United States, knowing that their collective historical and lived experiences are different from those ascribed to white people as a whole. At the same time, the privilege that comes with walking down the street with white skin cannot be denied and instead must be grappled with through the intersectional lenses that multicultural identity is viewed through.

There are limits to what I can say in this chapter. In a 2020 article titled "What Not to Say to Jews of Color Right Now," Generation Zer Aviva Davis writes, "What you should *never* do is use your platforms to speak for us. The last thing we need is another white savior. You may quote us with our permission, but the minute you try to describe how we are feeling or what we are thinking, you are automatically assuming you understand what it is like to be us."[23] As I write this, I acknowledge the privilege of my whiteness as I simultaneously claim the Jewish identity and collective experience that sets me apart from the white masses. My body holds both of these truths, just as the bodies of every member of the Jewish people, including those who have been born into this peoplehood and those who have joined it by choice, tell their own unique stories. For Jews of color, their reality is inherently different from mine, and I aim to lift up their voices rather than melding them into my own. This is a chapter that remains unfinished and is ready for other voices to add to it with their own stories.

NOTES

1. Schoenberg, S. (n.d.). Judaism: Ashkenazim. Jewish Virtual Library. Retrieved from https://www.jewishvirtuallibrary.org/ashkenazim.

2. Shkolnikova, S. (2011). The Jewfro grows up and out. *Moment Magazine.*

3. Kamalipour, Y. R., & Carilli, T. (1998). Media stereotypes of Jews. In *Cultural diversity and the U.S. media* (pp. 99–110). Albany: State University of New York Press.

4. Schrenk, B. (2007). "Cutting off your nose to spite your race": Jewish stereotypes, media images, cultural hybridity. *Shofar: An Interdisciplinary Journal of Jewish Studies, 25*(4), 18.

5. Leichtag Foundation (n.d.). Population of Jews of color is increasing in U.S., despite undercounting in population studies. Retrieved from https://leichtag.org/press-release-population-of-jews-of-color-is-increasing -in-u-s-despite-undercounting-in-population-studies

6. Alper, B. A., & Cooperman, A. (2021, May 11). 10 key findings about Jewish Americans. Pew Research Center. Retrieved from https://www.pewresearch.org/fact-tank/2021/05/11/10-key-findings-about -jewish-americans

7. Shalev, A. (2021, May 12). Without using the term, Pew survey unveils new data on US "Jews of color." *Times of Israel.* Retrieved from https://www.timesofisrael.com/without-using-the-term-pew-survey -unveils-new-data-on-us-jews-of-color

8. Burack, E. (2019, November 7). Everything you need to know about Tiffany Haddish's "Black Mitzvah." *Alma.* Retrieved from https://www .heyalma.com/everything-you-need-to-know-about-tiffany-haddishs -black-mitzvah

9. Burack, E. (2019, November 22). Tiffany Haddish loves being Jewish. We talked to her about it. *Alma*. Retrieved from https://www.heyalma.com/tiffany-haddish-loves-being-jewish-we-talked-to-her-about-it

10. Rubin, R. (2012, June 7). A nose dive for nose jobs. *Tablet*. Retrieved from https://www.tabletmag.com/sections/community/articles/a-nose-dive-for-nose-jobs

11. Konner, M. (2009). *The Jewish body*. New York: Schocken.

12. Schwartz, M. (2018, March 17). Nose jobs have declined 43% since 2000. We sniffed out why. Garage. Retrieved from https://garage.vice.com/en_us/article/bjyw3w/nose-jobs-have-declined-43-since-2000-we-sniffed-out-why

13. Fox, M. (2021, June 8). Are more teens getting nose jobs—and is TikTok to blame? The Forward. Retrieved from https://forward.com/culture/471005/are-more-teens-getting-nose-jobs-and-is-tiktok-to-blame

14. Mann, J. (2021, May 15). The danger of that #nosejob trend on TikTok—opinion. *Jerusalem Post*. Retrieved from https://www.jpost.com/j-spot/the-danger-of-that-nosejob-trend-on-tiktok-opinion-668223

15. Stewart, B., & Scanlan, Q. (2020, July 28). Perdue's campaign deletes ad that enlarges Jewish opponent's nose, insists it was an accident. ABC News. Retrieved from https://abcnews.go.com/Politics/perdues-campaign-deletes-ad-enlarges-jewish-opponents-nose/story?id=72039950

16. Sherwood, H. (2021, April 22). Synagogues and Jewish venues urged to avoid racial profiling in security searches. *The Guardian*. Retrieved from https://www.theguardian.com/uk-news/2021/apr/22/synagogues-and-jewish-venues-urged-to-avoid-racial-profiling-in-security-searches

17. Crary, D. (2020, January 15). Experts advise synagogues on use of armed security personnel. AP News. Retrieved from https://apnews.com/article/shootings-north-america-race-and-ethnicity-religion-47342f278c26f83fbefa8aab221e4183

18. Burton, N. (2018, November 6). As a Black Jew, I'm begging you: Don't arm your synagogue. *Alma*. Retrieved from https://www.heyalma.com/as-a-black-jew-im-begging-you-don't-arm-your-synagogue

19. Sales, B. (2020, June 1). "Defund the police" creates conflicts for security-conscious Jews. *New York Jewish Week*. Retrieved from https://jewishweek.timesofisrael.com/defund-the-police-creates-conflicts-for-security-conscious-jews

20. Banschick, M. (2012, April 3). Passover: Four sons—five characters. *Psychology Today*. Retrieved from https://www.psychologytoday

.com/us/blog/the-intelligent-divorce/201204/passover-four-sons-five
-characters

21. Intraub, S. (n.d.). Lessons from "The Four Children" of the seder. Reform Judaism. Retrieved from https://reformjudaism.org/lessons-four -children-seder

22. Lerner, M. (1993, May 18). The white issue: "Jews are not white." *Village Voice*. Retrieved from https://www.villagevoice.com/2019/07/25 /the-white-issue-jews-are-not-white

23. Davis, A. (2020, June 30). "What not to say to Jews of color right now." *Alma*. Retrieved from https://www.heyalma.com/what-not-to-say -to-jews-of-color-right-now

EIGHT

What about Mom and Dad?

I think teens push boundaries because their lives are so confusing: they want to know what will hold fast. The only way to find out is to push.

—Kathleen Bauer, *Before the Dawn*

"My mom is my best friend."

"I think my parents did a really great job raising my siblings and I."

"My kids know they can talk to me about anything."

"Everything is on the table in our house."

"My parent's generation is f—ed up. It's my generation's turn to fix things."

The years of adolescence and emerging adulthood are often seen as a time of pulling away from parents and caregiver figures. During the teenage years in particular, individuals are trying to figure out who they are apart from their families, and as a result, they try to separate from their families of origin. They are, consciously or subconsciously, fighting for autonomy, freedom, and input on the decisions that impact them.[1] Ultimately, they are observing their families, their friends, and others in the orbit of influencers they see and figuring out what they want their own identities to look like.

As in more universal areas of their lives—such as curfews, family obligations, chores and other commitments, and plans for the future—so, too, can the parent/adolescent relationship be complex with regard to Jewish identity. Generation Zers, on the whole, are close with their parents. They view their parents as primary role models and, when they picture their Jewish futures, regularly see iterations of reality that mirror the experiences that were offered to them growing up.

For the parents of Generation Zers, the uptick in antisemitism is often a cause for concern. The parents of Generation Zers, themselves mostly from Generation X, had different understandings of and experiences with antisemitism in their formative years. They have a unique perspective on the challenges facing their children, both with regard to antisemitism directly as well as in terms of the overall Jewish identities and journeys that their children will continue to embark on as they move into the next stages of their lives against the backdrop of the twenty-first century.

Alina is a Michigan-based mother of a thirteen-year-old boy and a ten-year-old girl. Her family, like more than half of non-Orthodox Jewish families,[2] identifies as multifaith, with her children being raised with elements of Catholicism and Judaism. "We wanted a united family structure. We have two people who very strongly identify with their respective faiths, so it would have been disingenuous for us to do anything else." In chapter 7, Alina was quoted on her desire to ensure that her children feel a sense of belonging to the Jewish people and the wholeness of their Jewish identities. She is proud of how comfortable her children are in Jewish spaces, particularly in their synagogue. "My kids slide on the marble banisters in the sanctuary. I love it. I believe that children's laughter makes a place sacred. I want them to feel that a synagogue is a space that's comfortable and safe for them."

Alina's most recent encounter with antisemitism came in the woods behind her house. While walking on a trail, she saw wood chips that had been arranged in the shape of a swastika. Despite the desire to wipe the symbol away and keep going, Alina followed the steps she knew were necessary—calling the police and making a report and informing the local Anti-Defamation League. While as a parent, Alina has the conviction to always be honest with her children, she was torn about how to broach the subject with them. "I want my kids to know [about antisemitism]. I don't want to be hiding things from them. But at the same time, in my childhood the 'they hate us' piece was ever-present, and I don't want to share that. I don't want them to be fearful in that way."

Nicki is a mother of three in North Carolina. While she's originally from Chicago, the majority of her adult life has been intentionally spent in small Jewish communities across the American South. She and her husband are both Jewish communal professionals, and they've found a shared love of the unique experience that Jewish life in smaller communities provides for them and their children. With a thirteen-year-old son and twin ten-year-old girls, Nicki is on a mission to create positive relationships with Judaism for her Generation Zers. "I want to make Judaism something that they *want* to be involved in instead of it being a burden on them. It should be something fun, reflective, and hands-on." For Nicki, the experience that summarizes her approach to Jewish life for her family is their recent Lag BaOmer[3] celebration. While the family built a bonfire and honored the holiday rituals, at the other end of the driveway was a big screen with the NFL draft playing. By bringing together Jewish experiences and secular fun, a sense of Judaism as something that her kids want and enjoy is fostered.

Growing up in small Jewish communities, Nicki's children have understood early on what it means to be members of a minority group, with the challenges that come with that designation. All three of her children have experienced proselytization from their non-Jewish peers. She remembers her son, then in elementary school, asking in the car, "Who is Jesus?" Her daughter, a budding social justice activist, has begun to internalize the reality of a complex world, and has asked heartbreaking questions. "How can people hate other people because of their religion? Will people hate me because I'm Jewish? Mommy, did we do something wrong?"

As a parent, Nicki tries to figure out how to find the balance between protecting her children from some of the cruelties of the world and making sure they know about its realities. When her son went on a civil rights trip to Birmingham, Alabama, for example, he came back and shared that they saw a "white costume with a hat" [Ku Klux Klan robe]. But he reassured his mother, "It's OK, because they're not around anymore." Nicki settled in for a difficult parenting conversation. "I didn't want to give him false hope. I needed to make him aware that antisemitism happens, and it happens around us." Her son subsequently had an experience while playing flag football where the opposing team made derogatory comments about Jews. While the respective school administrations stepped in and dealt with the incident, the lasting impact still happened. "It was the first time that he had a real, in-your-face moment of someone essentially saying 'You're a Jew, and [because of that] I hate you.'"

Nicki intentionally wears a Star of David necklace daily, and her husband wears a kippah. Usually, these symbols of Judaism are welcome, with people coming up to ask questions, or sometimes to say "Shalom," identifying themselves as fellow Jews. But there are other times, when

Nicki will slip her necklace into the collar of her shirt, and hand her husband a baseball cap before leaving the car. "It's not so much about our safety. But I worry about the kids and what they might experience." Nicki wants her children to be able to have difficult conversations about their Judaism as well as the rest of their lives and to be comfortable being Jewish wherever they end up in their lives.

For many of the parents of Generation Zers I spoke to, this sense of their children having a comfort with Judaism was paramount. Very few parents were inclined to give specific, measurable outcomes for what they wanted for their children's Jewish futures. The overarching themes, rather, centered around largely amorphous goals, with pride, a sense of ease in Jewish spaces and situations, and joy as oft-cited examples of a successfully connected Jewish adult. One father summed things up succinctly: "I hope that they find a community that is a Jewish space that welcomes them, where they're comfortable, and where they feel loved." For those parents, however, who bucked the trend and opted to give specifics regarding their hopes for the Jewish futures of their Generation Zers, the majority came from the more traditionally observant and Orthodox denominations of the community.

Lena is a Maryland-based mother of two daughters. She describes her family as "Conservadox" in terms of their Jewish observance, with her husband's family coming from an Orthodox background and her own being more secular. The melding of these two upbringings resulted in a traditionally Jewish household with adherence to the rules governing Shabbat and Jewish dietary practices and Jewish education being of paramount importance. When reflecting on the Jewish education and context that was provided to her now–twenty-somethings, she shared, "History and knowing where you come from is very important. So many kids are trying to find themselves and figure out who they are. It's good to ground kids in this history, to say that you're part of history, and you're not on your own."

In addition to instilling a sense of Jewish connection and pride, Lena focused on halacha, Jewish ritual laws and regulations, in terms of the values she emphasized to her family. "If you have different choices within reasonable boundaries, it's comforting. It's up to you to go out or come back, but I know my kids and I find it comforting to know that this is the way that we live, because of our heritage and our history." In the field of adolescent psychology, it has been found that setting boundaries is helpful for adolescents in particular. In various capacities, having firm boundaries teaches teens that they have responsibilities and that their actions have consequences. It sets them up to take their places in society, and the work-place, with the knowledge that there are limits and potential repercussions to behavioral choices.[4] Lena's philosophy of choices within boundaries extends not just to the practices she hopes her children will take on but also to their interpersonal relationships.

"We don't care about the gender of their future partners. But we would like for them to marry someone Jewish and to have a Jewish home." Both of Lena's children are currently dating non-Jewish partners, which has led to the parental question: Have you talked to your partner about your Judaism? This question of relationships and life partners as markers of Jewish identity and success is one that comes up within many questions on both individual and collective levels about what the Jewish future will manifest as.

Josh, the father of three Jewish Generation Zers in Illinois, shared what matters the most to his children in terms of their relationships and choices of partners. "They envision having Jewish kids, but not necessarily Jewish partners." It has been known for generations that intermarriage is on the rise in non-Orthodox Jewish communities. The 2020 Pew study on the American Jewish population notes that 61 percent of Jews who have gotten married since 2010 chose a non-Jewish spouse and that 82 percent of married Jews with at least one non-Jewish parent themselves have a non-Jewish spouse.[5] The majority of married Jews with children opt to raise their children Jewishly, albeit with more Jews married to Jews making this choice than Jews with non-Jewish partners.[6] No longer is intermarriage seen by many, particularly in the non-Orthodox world, as an unthinkable taboo. Instead, research conducted on millennial children of interfaith marriages as compared to previous generations has shown that younger Jews are more likely than their older counterparts to have been raised Jewish and to have received a formal Jewish education. As a result, they are more likely to identify as Jewish in adulthood, a development attributed to an increasingly welcoming Jewish community.[7]

The collective knowledge that having a non-Jewish partner does not necessarily correlate with a loss of Jewish identity for the next generation has led to greater levels of acceptance of intermarriage. In 1991, literary critic Leslie Fiedler wrote, "Not one of my own eight children has, at the present moment, a Jewish mate; nor for that matter do I. . . . In any case, there is no one to say kaddish [the Jewish mourning prayer] for me when I die. I am, in short, not just as I have long known, a minimal Jew—my Judaism nearly non-existent—but, as I have only recently become aware, a terminal one, the last of a four-thousand-year line."[8] In the 1990s, intermarriage was viewed as a failing of the community, with accusations flying: How can you (or, more accurately, we) have let this happen?

In the 2020s, the tides have turned. Among the parents of Generation Zers that were interviewed for this book, those who opined on the subject of their children's current or theoretical future partners were often uncomfortable and reluctant in doing so. Sometimes there was an air of hesitation, followed by a query: *Is it OK to say I'd like them to marry someone Jewish? Did other people say anything about this?* For others, there were clarifications. *I'm fine with whoever they end up with, but I hope that if they choose to have children, they'll raise them with Jewish identities. I support whatever choices my kids make.*

Many of the Generation Zers themselves were equally ambivalent about the religious identities of their potential future partners. *It's important to me to be Jewish, but if the person I end up with isn't, I feel like we'll have a lot to learn from each other. It's great if they're Jewish, but it's not a deal breaker either way.*

Generation Zers are being raised to be tolerant, open-minded individuals. They are the most racially and ethnically diverse demographic cohort that the United States has ever seen, with 48 percent identifying as part of communities of color.[9] They are also the most educated generation to date. As consumers, they differ from the generations that came before them. Ideologically, Generation Xers, those born between 1960 and 1979, were consumers of status, while millennials are consumers of experiences. Generation Z's main driver is the search for truth in both personal and communal forms. According to McKinsey & Company, "this generation feels comfortable not having only one way to be itself. Its search for authenticity generates greater freedom of expression and greater openness to understanding different kinds of people."[10]

Tolerance toward those who are different, however, does not always align with tolerance within one's own community. Aaron, a single father of four in Maryland, raised his children in an observant Jewish household. He described it as skewing toward Orthodox while eschewing hard-and-fast labels. However, as his children have left their home, each one in turn has moved away from connecting with Judaism. Aaron shared some of his frustrations with his emerging adult children regarding their Jewish identities. "They see Judaism as very much a light switch—like it's an on or off thing. Either you're Orthodox, or you're nothing. That's not how they were raised. We have some family that's observant and some not, so they grew up around people who were serious about their Judaism without being religious. But once they opted out of some parts of Judaism, they also felt like they were leaving the rest of it. I'm accused of being a hypocrite because I do some things but not everything. But that's what *most* Jews do."

Aaron and his children lived in Israel for several years during their childhood, later returning to the United States. He found that his children began pulling away from expressing their Jewish identities during their college years. "They started to distance themselves first regarding Israel so that way they wouldn't have to answer for it. They wanted to be accepted as liberals and progressives, and there's a sense that if you're any of those things, you can't support Israel. Judaism came next."

Brad, who in his work encounters many young adults, noted the psychological impact that the Jewish, and specifically Israel-focused, situation on many college campuses has on Generation Zers figuring out their identities. "Being on a college campus and being called a baby killer for being a Zionist is going to impact your mental health." Many parents, from all Jewish and political streams of ideology, view the college years as a watershed moment when it comes to their children's Jewish identities.

Dina, the mother of two college-aged Generation Zers, knew that from birth until age eighteen, she had done all that she could to empower her children as proud Jews. She and her husband instilled Jewish life and community as values in their family, choosing to live in an area with a large and robust Jewish population, and involving her children in synagogue, youth groups, and camp throughout their childhood. When it came to the college journey, the rule was that her children could only apply to schools that had a dedicated campus Hillel. This removed many schools that are only associated with citywide or regional branches of Hillel from contention, all with the goal of ensuring that her children would continue to feel supported and connected as Jews. But now, she's facing the next challenge in parenting Jewish emerging adults. "I worry about how they'll access Judaism postcollege. Will they make the effort to find a synagogue—or a havurah or something—where they'll continue to meet other Jewish people?"

The worries of Jewish parents are stereotypically well known, a stereotype that manifested as true during the interviews conducted for this book.

"I worry that my great-grandchildren won't be Jewish."

"I hope that they'll marry Jewish people, but I guess I'm out of date in saying that."

"My son's school was tagged with a swastika last summer, and he was the first person in our family to find out. I'm worried that antisemitism stopped being a concept and turned into something that we're actually confronting. He knows now that there are people out there who hate us as Jews because of their worldview, and that's a real thing."

"I'm worried they won't know the difference between opportunities for conversation and when to call out antisemitism."

"I'm worried about how they'll find the balance between being Jewish in a way that touches every area of their lives and being able to engage with people in the rest of the world."

The fears of parents are deeply real. They come from a place of love, of experience, of recognizing that their children are poised to inherit an imperfect world that they ultimately cannot adequately prepare them for. Because of the ever-changing reality that each new generation faces, parents are tasked with making decisions grounded in values that emerged from the past as ways to meet the challenges of a world that has yet to be defined.

The parent of two Generation Zers, one of whom identifies as nonbinary, shared, "I want them to have an internal moral, ethical, and philosophical framework for how they navigate the world. I think the Jewish framework was meaningful for me in terms of how I was raised, and I want to give that to them. I don't care how religious they are, but the sense of Jewish peoplehood and that this is their community to have as a foundation is what's important to me."

Each parent of a child, whether either or both of the parties (parent/child) are Jewish, will have a different sense of success when it comes to the individuals their children grow into and how they carry themselves in the world. When I work with the parents of Jewish Generation Zers, I feel the anxiety that comes with knowing that children can't be protected in perpetuity and that there is inevitable challenge, sadness, and hate in their future. Parents usually come to me for two services that I'm able to provide: reassurance and crisis management.

In my reassuring hat, I'm often asked to confirm that parents have done a good job and have laid a strong foundation for their kids so that, as they go out into the world, they'll be able to stand firm as Jews. They'll know who they are, and it'll make them better people. As we have seen throughout this book, and as we will particularly focus on in the next chapter, Jewish identity is often a fluid concept, depending on how and where it manifests. But for parents, worried about their kids and the future they're stepping toward, more concrete terms are often the most comfortable. *You did a great job. They'll be fine. Everything you're worried about isn't a big deal—they know what they need to know.* And many times, those things are true. But if Jewish education and Jewish identity haven't been conversations in a familial context for years, and these questions are asked only when the lurking presence of antisemitism rears its head, expectations are set that can't always be met.

There's no such thing as "too late" when it comes to the Jewish experience. In the Talmud, we learn about Rabbi Akiva, who is considered to be one of the greatest rabbinic sages of all time. Unlike many renowned rabbis and leaders, Rabbi Akiva did not come from an impressive lineage, nor did he have an elite education. Instead, his story teaches that he first learned how to read and began to study at the age of forty.[11] Many parents of Generation Zers get nervous and ask, *If my children didn't get involved in high school, are they "lost"?* And my answer is no. The entry points to Jewish engagement are lifelong and should not be pursued out of fear but rather out of love. If the "why" that is presented is that of the danger and rage that the world too often shows to Jews, it's not a particularly compelling reason for claiming something as a meaningful aspect of one's overall identity. But if the why is proactive and brings value and is modeled by the adult role models in the lives of Generation Zers, the pathways to success are endless.

NOTES

1. Gordon, S. (2019, August 13). How to allow independence and still keep your teen close. Very Well Family. Retrieved from https://www.very wellfamily.com/how-to-allow-teen-independence-and-still-keep-them -close-4165998

2. Pew Research Center (2021, May 11). Jewish Americans in 2020: Marriage, families, and children. Retrieved from https://www.pewforum .org/2021/05/11/marriage-families-and-children

3. Klagsbrun, F. (n.d.). What is Lag Ba'omer? My Jewish Learning. Retrieved from https://www.myjewishlearning.com/article/lag-baomer

4. Relate UK (n.d.). Setting boundaries for teenagers. Relate: The Relationship People. Retrieved from https://www.relate.org.uk/relation ship-help/help-family-life-and-parenting/parenting-teenagers/behaviour /setting-boundaries-teenagers

5. Pew Research Center, Jewish Americans in 2020.

6. Smith, T. (n.d.). The missing 2020 Pew study headlines. 18 Doors. Retrieved from https://18doors.org/the-missing-2020-pew-study-headlines

7. Sasson, T., Aronson, J. K., Chertok, F., Kadushin, C., & Saxe, L. (2017). Millennial children of intermarriage: Religious upbringing, identification, and behavior among children of Jewish and non-Jewish parents. *Contemporary Jewry, 37*, pp. 99–123. Retrieved from https://doi.org/10.1007/s12397-017-9202-0

8. Lebovic, M. (2019, July 12). When American Jews described their own intermarriage as a "second Holocaust." *Times of Israel*. Retrieved from https://www.timesofisrael.com/when-american-jews-described-their-own-intermarriage-as-a-second-holocaust

9. Wang, H. L. (2018, November 15). Generation Z is the most racially and ethnically diverse yet. NPR. Retrieved from https://www.npr.org/2018/11/15/668106376/generation-z-is-the-most-racially-and-ethnically-diverse-yet

10. Francis, T., & Hoefel, F. (2018, November 12). "True Gen": Generation Z and its implications for companies. McKinsey & Company. Retrieved from https://www.mckinsey.com/industries/consumer-packaged-goods/our-insights/true-gen-generation-z-and-its-implications-for-companies

11. Ratzabi, H. (n.d.). Who was Rabbi Akiva? My Jewish Learning. Retrieved from https://www.myjewishlearning.com/article/rabbi-akiba

NINE

Proud but Uncertain: Jewish Identity and Self Definitions

You have to be your own person. You can't let people's opinions determine how you think about yourself. There's a difference between identity and self-identity.

—Amy Tan

"The reason why identity is important, particularly when you are a minority, is that defining your own identity is to state your personal and communal right to self-determination. It ensures the fusion of your personal and social external identities."[1] Ben Freeman, the author of *Jewish Pride: Rebuilding a People*, explores Jewish identity through the lens of the LGBTQ Pride movement. By using the language and imagery imbued by his intersectional identity, Freeman calls upon Jews of all ages, but particularly young Jews, to view their Jewish identities through active, rather than passive, lenses. It's relatively easy to know that one is Jewish. It's something that one is told, by virtue of one's birth into a Jewish family or via an intentional conversion process. But to know exactly what being Jewish means, and how it manifests in a valuable way along one's life journey, is a far more complex process. Having a strong Jewish identity is regularly listed among the ideal outcomes for participants in Jewish educational and cultural programs. But understanding what this broad, often amorphous, term looks like in real time is a challenge for practitioners and participants inside and outside of Jewish spaces.

Identity formation, the process by which individuals develop clear and unique views of themselves and their respective identities, comes to a critical stage during the years of adolescence and emerging adulthood. Generation Zers span these respective developmental stages and often find themselves at pivot points and moments of change as they grapple with questions of identity. Developmental psychologist Erik Erikson's theory of development centers around the idea that at each stage of life, there is a crisis that must be resolved in order for the person to progress to the next stage. During adolescence, the crisis is that of Identity versus role confusion.[2] In this stage, adolescents are faced with existential questions: Who am I? What can I be/do? The goal, according to Erikson, is for adolescents to reach the headspace of identity achievement, understanding who they are as unique persons. This process is influenced by everything—family, peers, environment, and sociocultural context as well as personal abilities and tendencies.

While adolescents may work to develop an inner sense of self that is unique to them as individuals, particularly as members of a minority group, Jewish Generation Zers are also tasked with building an affinity with their social identities. Social identity is the portion of an individual's self-concept that is derived from membership in a relevant social group[3]—in this case, the Jewish community. For many young Jews, if and how they will identify with Judaism in an active or visible way is an active choice, while for others, how they identify comes from instinct and instilled familial and peer-group influences.

Jewish identity in the United States is teasingly complex. On the surface, it appears straightforward: Does a person connect with what it means to be Jewish? But in reality, there are countless minutiae that feed into the overall development of what a strong Jewish identity looks like and how it manifests. In the 2013 Pew Report on the American Jewish community, it was noted that

> U.S. Jews see being Jewish as more of a matter of ancestry, culture and values than of religious observance. Six-in-ten say, for example, that being Jewish is *mainly* a matter of culture or ancestry, compared with 15 percent who say it is mainly a matter of religion. Roughly seven-in-ten say remembering the Holocaust and leading an ethical life are essential to what it means to them to be Jewish, while far fewer say observing Jewish law is a central component of their Jewish identity. And two-thirds of Jews say that a person can be Jewish even if he or she does not believe in God.[4]

If Jewish identity cannot be defined by Jewish laws or the beliefs of the majority of Jews and, instead, culture and ethics are seen as the cornerstones of the Jewish experience, how that translates to Generation Zers requires different metrics and measurements. In a 2019 survey of Jewish Generation Z, it was found that largely, Generation Zers agree with the perspectives of older generations when it comes to culture being the main driver of Jewish identity. Many teens expressed a greater affinity for Jewish culture than for traditional religious engagement,[5] and teens did not feel bound by religious denominations when it came to how they express their Judaism. However, when it comes to what it means to be a minority group in the United States, feelings and personal preferences are not all that need to be taken into account.

Title VI of the Civil Rights Act prohibits discrimination in programs receiving federal support on the basis of "race, color, or national origin" but not religion.[6] If Jews are only identified as a religion, then they are not covered by Title VI and can be discriminated against by federally funded programs. However, when discrimination against Jews, as well as Muslims or Sikhs, is based on "the group's actual or perceived ancestry or ethnic characteristics" or "actual or perceived citizenship or residency in a country whose residents share a dominant religion or a distinct religious identity," then that discrimination does fall under Title VI. Antisemitic discrimination is unlawful under Title VI to the extent that it targets Jews as a racial or national group.[7]

During the Trump presidency, an executive order[8] was passed that called on government departments enforcing Title VI to adopt the International Holocaust Remembrance Alliance definition of antisemitism:[9] "Antisemitism is a certain perception of Jews, which may be expressed as hatred toward Jews. Rhetorical and physical manifestations of antisemitism are directed toward Jewish or non-Jewish individuals and/or their property, toward Jewish community institutions and religious facilities." The announcement of the executive order, and the idea that Jews would be included as a nationality, triggered a tremendous backlash within the American Jewish community. Critics perceived the order as denying the Americanness of American Jews by separating them into their own nation.[10] For American Jews to be made to feel that their Judaism sets them apart from their Americanism is seen as a threat, triggering fears about never being accepted and always being "other."

Jewish identity is many things. It's connecting with the global Jewish people. It's participating in the Jewish religion. It's internalizing aspects of Jewish culture. It's taking ownership of Jewish rituals and traditions and making choices through a Jewish lens. For Generation Z, Jewish identity is often a source of pride, and it manifests through a variety of means. It is not bound by institutions or actions that previous generations would have used as barometers of identification. Instead, individuals and the generation as a whole are engaged in the process of ethnic identity development[11] and self-actualization.

Jewish identity, as with all identities, is in flux in the twenty-first century. Between 1791 and 1945, Jews in countries across Europe went through the process of emancipation. The emancipation of Jewish communities brought Jews to a recognized state of equality as citizens and led to integration into civil society.[12] The emancipation created a new definition for what Jews were thought of as, and it upended what Jewish life looked like. No longer were Jews subject to living in the ghettos and shtetls that had defined the European Jewish experience, and instead, they, as individuals and a collective, needed to rediscover what connecting with Judaism looked like once it was no longer societally enforced. In the United States of the 2020s, a new reckoning with what Jewish life can and should look like is emerging.

Andrés Spokoiny, the president and CEO of the Jewish Funders Network, wrote the following in response to the 2020 Pew Report on the American Jewish community:

> The changes in Jewish life and patterns of affiliation observed by Pew all stem from one basic reality: We live in a time of radical free choice and individual hyper-empowerment. Today, individuals don't receive their identity from their family, but they build it through their individual choices. The individual, and not the collective, is at the center of society, and that individual has more power than ever to carve her own path. Embracing the basic fact that people today have more freedom and power *as individuals* than ever before in human history is key to understanding much of Pew. What it observes is not a series of Jewish communal failures—although there certainly are some—but a complex of radical free choice that affects the way in which Jews and non-Jews alike build their identities.[13]

In this age of complete personalization, the experience of Generation Zers is in many ways unique. Traditional Judaism, and traditional expressions of Jewish life, tend to thrive on the collective. Certain central Jewish prayers cannot be said without a quorum of ten. Jewish life-cycle events, learning styles, and experiences, are predicated on being part of a community. And yet, it is known that millennials and Generation Zers connect as individuals, practicing unbundling[14] and disassociating themselves from institutional affiliations. Judaism, therefore, has become more of a personal endeavor, and what it means to identify with it is a changing concept.

Speaking to Jewish Generation Zers, there are a few trends that tend to emerge. There are the stereotypes of Generation Z that hold true—self-described smartphone addictions, a drive to succeed, a sense of the importance of authenticity and connection when it comes to how they affiliate and the choices they make.[15] And for Jewish Generation Zers in particular, there's a unique set of Jewish understandings and baggage that have shaped their experiences to date and that inform the worldviews that characterize this cohort. Like their millennial counterparts, Generation Zers are known for prioritizing universalism over particularism and for largely identifying with progressive values and movements.[16] Against this backdrop, the specificity that comes with a strong Jewish affiliation can feel almost countercultural. It's not in keeping with the status quo of being a teenager or emerging adult[17] in 2020 to adhere to particular organizational affiliations that tend to characterize religious observance, so for those who do choose to claim their Judaism, to do so is most often an intentional act.

While being Jewish is typically something that one is born into or converts to later in life, in the United States of the twenty-first century, it's not a given that one acts on this identifying factor in any way. Outside of Orthodox Judaism, where there is increased familial and societal pressure to adhere to Jewish religious observance and cultural norms, many Jewish families do not prioritize ongoing, regular interaction with this facet of their identities for their teens. There is a value placed on the *b'nai mitzvah* experience, but beyond that adolescent rite of passage, many families tend to leave the choice about whether to continue with Jewish activities and practices up to their children. Against a backdrop of competing priorities and opportunities, from sports to socializing with friends to the ever-increasing pressure of the college résumé and upcoming admissions process, it is easy to understand why teens may not list Jewish activities at the top of their to-do lists (if they're mentioned at all). But while the majority of teens may not participate in formal Jewish experiences, such as youth groups, camps, or religious schools, and may not even partake in traditional Jewish practices outside of holidays spent with family, they continue to identify Jewishly and do so proudly.

In my work with Jewish high schoolers across the country, I've had the opportunity to speak to teens of every denominational affiliation and from families with varying relationships with the organized Jewish community. Many of the teens have chosen to opt out of Jewish life on paper. You won't find them in traditional Jewish spaces. But when these teens talk about their Judaism, it's more often than not in the same terms as those teens who are involved. There are shared threads of the American Jewish experience, with teens finding a sense of pride in their Jewish identities and feeling motivation to improve the world as a result of their Jewish upbringings, ancestry, and behavioral norms.

Genna, a public-school student from Maryland, describes her Jewish identity by saying, "Being Jewish is being really thoughtful and kind to others. When you learn about Judaism, you learn that they've gone through a lot of hardships in their history, and the whole point of the Torah is that you need to still be nice to others, no matter what they do to you." Her older brother, Matt, expanded on that definition. "To be Jewish is to be part of a smaller community and to have pride in having bounced back through hundreds of years of prejudice and oppression. I have a lot of pride in that history."

Hallie's Jewish identity centers around Shabbat. But, she's quick to clarify, her family doesn't celebrate Shabbat in the "traditional" sense. While they do belong to a Conservative synagogue, since her bat mitzvah she's only attended sporadically on holidays or for family celebrations. Hallie and her younger brother are both proud of their Judaism and love inviting friends, both Jewish and non-Jewish, over for Shabbat dinners. Every Friday night, her family hosts Shabbat dinners for friends and community members, kicking off a twenty-four-hour period that feels intentionally separate from the rest of the week. Recently, traditions such as "tech-free Shabbat" have caught on for Jewish and non-Jewish families alike. People have found that "tech Shabbat allows you to take a break and remember an era when spending time on things that take time was part of the pleasure."[18]

For Hallie's family, Shabbat is a time when everything they do is separate from the norm of the rest of the week. "I don't do my homework, but I work on art projects. I take walks around the neighborhood with my friends. And my mom always makes a meal that she knows we're all going to love. We're together as a family, and it's just the most special time of the week. I hope I'm able to continue having some kind of Shabbat practice in college. I know in some ways it'll be easy because I'll have a Hillel, but

I'm sure I'll have friends who aren't Jewish or who don't do Shabbat, and I'll probably want to go out with them too. So I'm not sure what it'll look like once I'm not at home."

For Shira, the mother of five Generation Zers, a deep sense of pride came when she first observed one of her sons in a non-Jewish social setting. Her son began playing pickup basketball with other teenage boys in their neighborhood. None of them was identifiably Jewish. "I was surprised that I never saw him without his kippah. But it's a part of who he is, so I guess he never felt like he needed to take it off to fit in. I wonder what he, and the rest of my kids, will come up against as they encounter the larger world outside of our Jewish bubble. Not just antisemitism, but all the hates."

Meghan, the mother of three Generation Zers in Virginia, noted that her children all have strong Jewish identities. "Our kids are growing up in a diverse world. They're comfortable with different kinds of people, and that's great. But I don't want them to lose sight of what makes their own identities special." Her middle schooler has a particularly diverse group of friends, which has led to some instances of antisemitism. "Sometimes he'll be picked on—just like everyone else gets their turn in the group— but when it's his turn, it's about his Judaism. Like if he falls when they're playing soccer, it's 'Jew, get up!' " Nevertheless, he's proud of his Judaism and doesn't see this as offensive. He's part of a diverse community and feels very connected to that space while remaining bonded to his Jewish identity. But like his siblings, "he's much more outward looking."

A common thread when it comes to conversations about Jewish identity is that of food and the ritual observances centered around food in the Jewish tradition. Collectively referred to as kashrut or keeping kosher, the rules around Jewish dietary practices range from the well known (no pork[19]) to the humane (You shall not boil a kid in its mother's milk[20]) to the confusing (chicken now counts as meat but didn't always[21]). Today, keeping kosher manifests differently for many non–Orthodox Jewish families. There are some who keep strictly kosher homes but who are comfortable eating nonkosher food outside of the home. Others may subscribe to the philosophy of ethical kashrut, which focuses more on ensuring the Jewish dietary laws and practices they abide by are ones that align with environmentalist best practices and fair labor laws.[22] And even leaving aside the rules aspect, there are countless questions when it comes to Jews and food. What "counts" as a Jewish food? Can Jews still claim bagels now that they have gained solid footing in the American mainstream? When it comes to Israeli foods that have taken the world by storm, such as the breakfast egg dish shakshuka,[23] do they qualify as Jewish if their origins are in North African cuisine?

As the Jewish community becomes increasingly diverse, some of these questions are no longer so lighthearted. For Jews of non-Ashkenazi backgrounds, whose traditional familial dishes are neither the ones touted by Seinfeld nor the ones that get movies made about them (like Seth Rogen's *An American Pickle*), it's easy for the implicit erasure to feel othering and hurtful. And even for those Jews whose family backgrounds are thought of as mainstream, questions of food often come to a head when it comes to exploring what it means to socialize, behave, and ultimately live engaged Jewish lives.

Vanessa's son recently celebrated his bar mitzvah. As this coming-of-age ceremony traditionally marks the tradition from childhood into the responsibilities of Jewish adulthood, he has been eager to flex the muscles of making his own Jewish choices. As a devout carnivore, his first act as an "official" Jewish adult was to question the strictly kosher home he grew up in. Now that he's a Jewish adult, he wonders if he still has to keep kosher.

Kathy is raising her Generation Zers in a strictly kosher home as well. But outside of the house, things are a little more lax. What started as something that the family engaged in only when traveling—the better to sample the best of local cuisines—became an ongoing practice outside the home. "Outside, we eat whatever. But inside, we are 100 percent kosher. So the kids [ages eleven and fourteen] spend a lot of time asking, 'Why can't we eat the things we want at home?'" Meghan, who has three Generation Zers, knows that growing up, her kids also chafed against the restrictions of their kosher home. They were the only family in their social circles that kept kosher, and her kids longed to be just like everyone else.

Lena lives outside of Washington, DC. Growing up, she came from a secular Jewish family, but when she married her husband, who was raised in a more traditional environment, the pair came to the decision to live a largely observant Jewish lifestyle, which, of course, includes keeping kosher. About this decision, Lena said, "It's really important to raise children with ritual, with boundaries, and with rules. Judaism is beautiful. There's a rhythm to life and it's predictable, and the rituals are beautiful and they align with our senses. And it's really important for children to grow up with that kind of structure—even if they don't keep it for themselves later on, they can take it with them and make it whatever they want."

What has been striking about the extent to which the varieties of kosher observance were mentioned in the research for this book is that not once did I ask a question about Jewish dietary practices or food in general. The majority of these conversations came about in response to the queries, "Tell me about your Jewish journey" and "What role does Judaism play in your/ your family's life?" For people to be drawn immediately to food when the entire breadth and depth of their Jewish experiences could potentially have been on the table for discussion is demonstrative of the primacy of place that food has in our identities. Michael Twitty, whose book *Kosher Soul* highlights his experience as an African American Jewish culinary historian and educator, writes, "In Jewish cooking, you have foods dictated by text, food that the Torah talks about. Then you have foods that speak to the land of Israel and what grows there. Then you have foods that come from the places we have been, from our diaspora. And then there is identity cooking. The foods that are tied up with your sense of self and the place you are in, where you are and how you connect to that place."[24] Claude Fischler describes the phenomenon as follows: "Food is central to our sense of identity. The way any given group eats helps it assert its diversity, hierarchy and organisation, but also, at the same time, both its oneness and the otherness of whoever eats differently. Food is also central to the individual identity, in that any given human individual is constructed, biologically, psychologically, and socially by the foods he/she chooses to incorporate."[25]

In the 2020 Pew Report on the American Jewish community, it was found that 72 percent of American Jews engage in the cultural activity of cooking Jewish food, the highest-ranked choice in the "Jewish culture" section of the report. While what qualifies as Jewish food within the parameters of the question is not clear, the fact that nearly three-quarters of American Jews think about Jewish food when they think about Jewish culture demonstrates the pervasiveness of food in the American Jewish experience. Each Jewish individual and each smaller Jewish community that makes up the collective have the capacity to harness food to signal their identities and to connect with them. Jewish social customs surrounding food have evolved over time, in particular related to kosher food, with anecdotes abounding about Jews avoiding accompanying their nonkosher steaks with milk, and the rise of kosher-style food.[26] While for many non-Orthodox Jews, it is not necessarily the biblical injunction that guides their dietary choices; the affinity toward what is seen as a cornerstone of Jewish identity cannot be denied.

Elisheva, the Jewish and Romani Generation Zer from Ohio, grew up knowing that her mother was Jewish but not necessarily having a strong sense of understanding of what that meant. Her upbringing was decidedly secular with a few ingrained traditions built in. "We never took flowers to a grave. We always placed pebbles on the headstones." This classic Jewish practice of mourning and honoring the dead aside,[27] Elisheva's biggest Jewish connection for a time manifested in her desire to get Rebecca Rubin, the Jewish American Girl doll released in 2009.[28] The American Girl franchise was created by Pleasant Company in 1986 and portrays adolescent girls from a variety of ethnicities, faiths, social classes, and backgrounds from various time periods throughout history. Each doll comes with an accompanying series of books, providing a glimpse into her time period and challenges, allowing the target audience of contemporary girls to connect with figures from the past as peers and potential role models.

Rebecca Rubin is the tenth historical character in the series. She is a Russian Jewish girl whose parents and grandparents immigrated to the Lower East Side of New York City—a typical Jewish story. She dreams of becoming an actress and, throughout her books, deals with issues of assimilation while remaining connected to her religious and cultural traditions. Rebecca's impact on modern Jewish American girls, who for the first time were able to see themselves in the iconic series portraying key points in American history, has been analyzed, with largely favorable outcomes.[29] Rebecca's immigrant story is familiar, but not stereotypical, and places her Jewishness into the context of a complex life story that fits into the broader American narrative.

As Elisheva learned more about Judaism in the context of world religions as a whole, she began to question her mother. She asked why certain traditions that she read about, like Shabbat, were not part of her routine and upbringing. And on a class trip to Philadelphia as a high school senior, she visited the National Museum of American Jewish History. There she saw a picture of a mother/daughter pair that she felt bore resemblance to herself and her own mother. "I took it as a sign. I can't run from this, and I need to know more about my culture and my family." Elisheva went down the rabbit hole of genealogical research while simultaneously exploring what it meant for her to take on Jewish traditions and customs in ways that felt personally meaningful for the first time. Today, her eclectic practices feel deeply authentic to her. "I keep Shabbat, but nontraditionally. I don't always eat kosher in my day-to-day life, but I *always* keep kosher on Shabbat. I light candles, and I try to shut my phone and meditate. I make it into a self-care evening."

While Elisheva is deeply connected with her Jewish identity and expresses it, her upbringing outside of Jewish institutions and standard norms of practice still sometimes keeps her on the outside of certain Jewish spaces. "Sometimes I feel like I'm not Jewish enough. I'm in a group chat with other Jewish content creators on TikTok, but I don't fit in. Everyone talks about going to camp and Hebrew school, and there are these bonds that I'm not part of because I didn't do any of that." As Elisheva grapples with how her Jewish identity fits into the larger landscape of her peers and connections with Jewish institutions and spaces, she feels connected to portrayals of nontraditional Judaism that have become increasingly popular in media and popular culture.

Rob, the Texas-based college student we met earlier, grew up aware of his status as part of a small minority in the heart of the Bible Belt. He was one of three Jews in his elementary school, along with his brother and the fifth-grade teacher. In high school, once his brother graduated, he alone represented the Jewish people. He is succinct in describing the foundation of his Jewish identity. "I see Judaism as bringing people together to eat and to argue." Rob grew up in a Reform Jewish household and counts his experience studying abroad in Israel in high school as the pivot point in taking charge of his own Jewish journey. His Jewish priorities lay in the area of community cultivation. "Judaism is about the community. I don't give a flippity flap about the prayers or what the holidays are for, but really about what they represent and how they bring us together." His pride in his Jewish identity has given him the strength to stand up for himself in the face of the antisemitism that he has experienced since childhood.

In many ways, Rob's encounters with antisemitism have served to keep him isolated from the rest of his community. "I never tell people about my antisemitism, because it's happened since elementary school and I should be used to it. And the desire to hide it comes from a feeling like a lot of other people have it a lot worse, so I shouldn't complain." He also intentionally gives credit to his encounters with antisemitism and hatred as motivating him to not only stand up for himself, or for the Jewish community, but to be an ally to others as well. "It's only when strangers become neighbors and start to help that we can make a difference. Antisemitism makes me more likely to stand up for others. My teachers saw the things that happened to me and did nothing about it. So even though it wasn't their fault, it kind of was. And now I know that you can't just stand up for yourself. You have to stand up for others for change to happen."

This kind of call to action and sense of purpose is demonstrative of the dual nature of Jewish identity for many Jewish Generation Zers. There is a sense of internal pride, connection, and peoplehood. And at the same time, there is a prioritization of looking externally and being of service to the needs of the wider community. Jewish tradition calls this urge toward justice *tikkun olam*. Tikkun olam, which literally translates to "repairing the world," is a concept within Judaism that has ancient roots but has contemporarily come to mean Jewish social justice.[30] Tikkun olam has become a connection point for many young Jews, particularly those who connect with progressive and liberal social and political values, and has in many ways permeated the American Jewish experience and vernacular.[31] It has come to be the rationale for the belief that Jews are responsible not only for creating a model society internally among themselves but also for the welfare of the societies in which they live and the global community as a whole.

In the Jewish mystical tradition of Kabbalah, there is a story about the creation of the universe. Prior to creation, the light of God filled all of existence, but in order to create the world and all it would contain, God contracted, creating figurative empty space for the world to fill in. The parts of the divine presence that contracted became vessels of light that ultimately shattered. After the shattering, the sparks of light dispersed throughout the world, with each human being becoming a new kind of vessel for this divine light. Only by engaging in acts to repair the world can the lights once again be gathered, restoring the sacredness of the universe, according to the Lurianic Kabbalah tradition.[32] While the majority of liberal Jewish Generation Zers do not necessarily have the vocabulary and context to recount the intricacies of Jewish mystical thought, the cultural inheritance of tikkun olam and the mission of finding the sparks in each human being have deeply resonated across denominations and practices. Amanda Berman, the Zioness founder and executive director, noted, "We [Jews] exist in this world to pursue justice."

Arielle, the Connecticut-based Instagram content creator, highlights her favorite aspect of Judaism as "Judaism is all about seeking knowledge and asking questions." A lifelong learner and explorer of Judaism, Arielle started out in a Jewish day school but entered middle school as one of the only Jews in her school. She identifies as a Conservative Jew, an ally, and an activist. Her direct experiences of antisemitism have been subtle. She's been told her nose "looks Jewish" and has done a great deal of soul-searching about how her Judaism and her white privilege intersect. Ultimately, her Judaism is a source of pride, connected to the breadth and longevity of Jewish history. "We're still here. We're thriving and adapting in every new place. We create new languages, like Yiddish and Ladino, finding ways to benefit and contribute. We build something everywhere we go."

For individuals of every demographic cohort, identity is an intersectional concept and reality. All individuals move through the world and develop a worldview, based on the lived experiences they have in relation to their gender, race, color, sexual orientation, and of course, religion. For Jewish Generation Zers, diversity is increasing in all of these regards. In the 2020 Pew report on the American Jewish population, it was found that while overall 8 percent of Jews identify as part of a racial or ethnic category other than non-Hispanic white, among those ages 18–29, the number grows to 15 percent. Twenty-nine percent of individuals in this category, which includes both Generation Z and the youngest of the millennials, live in households in which at least one adult or child is Black, Hispanic, Asian, some other nonwhite race or ethnicity, or multiracial.[33] While this statistic obviously demonstrates the increasing diversity of the American Jewish population, it also provides the backdrop for the increased awareness of white Jewish Americans about their numerous identities as well.

Mara, the SUNY Binghamton freshman from Michigan, noted, "I don't have to negotiate contrasting identities [like others do] because I'm a white Jew." Melinda, a Washington, DC, area–based parent of a Generation Zer, delved further into the way that race has taken on new importance for Jews of this demographic cohort. "Generation Z is the first generation of Jews to fully perceive themselves as white. For those who identify as white, it's not a conflict. That's how they're perceived by society. And for my generation, that wasn't a thing. We felt like we were something else—not exactly another race, but something different."

How whiteness and Jewish identity connect is becoming an ever-increasingly complex topic. It brings up questions about privilege and responsibility. Lisa, who works in the field of Holocaust education, brought up a dilemma faced by many white Jewish Generation Zers. "Antisemitism seems like such a lesser problem than being Black in the United States today. But at the same time, they know it's on the rise. So the question becomes, How do I square these things and feel like a good white person?" When speaking to Jews of earlier generations, this question is not raised in the same way. Many Jews acknowledge that despite being minorities and being discriminated against historically, they still retain the comparative advantages of white privilege[34] and the benefits derived from presenting as white in American society and in the world as a whole. At the same time, there are those who push back on being seen as part of the largely Christian, hegemonic white masses. These individuals note that the collective experience of Judaism and the identity-based baggage that comes with it constitute not just a religion but an ethnicity, and that lumping them together as white people is a disservice and an erasure of their lived experiences.

While the desire generally and reasonably is for Jewish identity to be a positive experience—forged within the individual and based on experiences as part of a collective—it cannot be denied that antisemitism and the stereotypes it espouses have seeped into the American Jewish psyche, often impacting how Jews see themselves. Brad, who researches and works in the combatting antisemitism space, described the phenomenon as the "built-in self-preservation mechanism of antisemitism." He continued:

> If you accept the logic of antisemitism that says Jews are rich, powerful, and privileged, the obvious question is how can such a group be oppressed? Antisemitism includes ideas that Jews are loud, whiny, complainers, so to show that we are *not* that, we'll oftentimes downplay our own oppression. We'll deprioritize it in order to show that we are good members of society. We don't put the interests of Israel first, for example, which is one of the most common antisemitic stereotypes in the world today, that Jews are more loyal to Israel than to whichever country they live in. We play out these behaviors to show that we are not the stereotype, to show that we try to be allies rather than centering ourselves. We want to show that we care about others. Another common idea is that Jews don't care about anyone other than their own kind. So we try to play the role of the "good Jew."

The complexities of being a minority, particularly as a member of a "model minority" group,[35] can permeate every aspect of identity, including what success looks like for members of the group once they come of age. When I've spoken to Jewish educators about what success looks like for alumni of their programs, and how they know they've done their job well, one of the most common themes is having alumni who are proud to be Jewish and who are comfortable in Jewish spaces. For Jewish Generation Zers, the sense of pride is apparent. But the spaces in which these young people spend their time Jewishly are not necessarily limited to the Jewish community.

Addison, the military mother with two children, noted that her Generation Z–aged son has a strong sense of his Jewish identity, as well as an overall strong sense of self. "He's been criticized by his peers for not being Christian, and for being somehow 'other.' We tend to live in places without a lot of other Jews. So sometimes it's antisemitism, but sometimes it's just the unknown. He has the burden of explaining to his classmates what

Judaism is. Why is he not eating a ham sandwich or not eating bread for eight days in the Spring, and saying, 'I'm Jewish'—whatever that means?" Food and holidays are a big part of how Judaism is first understood by many younger children. They become aware of the sense of being different, of knowing that Christmas, for example, is "not mine," and later they develop relationships with the traditions and collective experiences that they themselves have inherited.

Allyson, the parent of three Generation Zers based in Pennsylvania, described success in largely universalist terms. "Having a connection and a feeling of identity right now is important for all kids. They all need to feel some kind of belonging and to know that they fit in some place. It's so meaningful to have that." The importance of being part of a community and having a place within the larger world cannot be overstated, particularly during the challenging years of adolescence and emerging adulthood. Allyson further continued that for her Generation Zers, what success looks like for their Jewish identities as they come of age is inextricably linked to the overall success of the country and environment that they're being raised within. "Right now, we're at a crossroads as a country, and I'm concerned about what ideals are embraced nationally. It could become a lot harder for any of us who aren't old, white, Christian males . . . it could be harder for them to embrace who they are if they see more and more people who don't. If they're bombarded by messages that who and what they are is wrong, it's not accepted, and you're hated for who you are, you can't help but absorb it. I hope my kids understand what's normal and this doesn't become their normal."

Jess, the New Jersey–based social worker that we met in chapter 2, was a bit of an outlier. She shared that she would only marry a Jewish partner while acknowledging that in her social circles, that made her something of an anomaly. "Most of my friends see being Jewish as just a culture. But I see it as my duty to keep the religion going too." Bailey, the New York-based college student, spoke in similar terms about the responsibility she feels in making the intentional choice to place importance on having a Jewish family while keeping the question of her potential future partner's identity open. "I want to have a Jewish family because I see the history disappearing, and I don't want to see this culture and history vanish for good."

In *Mazel Tov: The Story of My Extraordinary Friendship with an Orthodox Jewish Family,* Belgian writer J. S. Margot recounts her experiences working for an Orthodox Jewish family, including quirks, idiosyncrasies, and heartwarming moments. In one interlude, Margot describes a conversation that she had with one of the sons in the family she worked for. In a tutoring session, the duo were discussing languages, and the author posed the question: What is your native language?

> French, perhaps. Hebrew, *Ivrit*, to an extent. But later my native language will be English or American.
>
> Your native language is the language of where you were born, you can't change it "later"!
>
> I was born in Judaism.[36]

This sense of Jewishness as being its own location, culture, and encompassing reality in many ways speaks to a bygone era. For the majority of history, being Jewish required no intentionality, no choices. You simply *were.* You were born into a Jewish family, the rhythms of your life were governed by the Jewish calendar of holidays and life-cycle events, and Jewish community defined your circle. Of course, the nostalgia of the past cannot authentically be viewed through rose-colored glasses. Being Jewish all too often also meant rules that restricted your profession and freedom of movement. You had to live in fear of humiliation, physical harm, and even death stemming from identifying, willingly or not, with the Jewish people. But regardless, the reality was the same. Jewish identity was unquestioned.

For Generation Zers, on the other hand, anything and everything can be and often is up for debate. Jewish identity may not be as inextricable as the skin that holds each of us together. For some, it may be more analogous to an article of clothing that can be taken on and off when a moment calls for one's Jewish self, as opposed to or in addition to another facet of an intersectional personality. For still others, Judaism is a pair of glasses, something still intentionally put on, providing the lens through which they are able to see the world more clearly and meaningfully. In all of these cases, Jewish identity is in flux. While the core may be unchanging, how it manifests throughout a lifetime is fluid and complex.

Science fiction author Donald Kingsbury wrote, "Tradition is a set of solutions for which we have forgotten the problems." Jewish identity, in the eyes of Generation Zers as well as many of the parents and educators who have partnered with them in shaping their experiences to date, is best expressed through traditions. From the ancient rituals of holidays to modern rites of passage, Jewish identity is marked by inner beliefs and affinities as well as by outward-facing actions. In many cases, the traditions that emerged, either historically or in recent personal and collective memory, did so as a response to antisemitism and identification as a minority group. The well-known holidays of Passover, Purim, and Chanukah are stories that are retold each year about the Jewish people overcoming various forms of oppression and have come to mark the seasonal calendar of Jewish experiences. Likewise, more modern traditions that provide meaning and ritual to young Jews, such as summer camp, Israel experiences, and the routines of Jewish socialization, at their core stem from reactions to antisemitism. And yet, as Kingsbury alluded, Generation Zers, active participants and recipients of all of these experiences, are often unaware of this context.

The traditions were originally meant to ensure that stories and legacies of the past would be retained in future generations. Each holiday is designed in order to engage children, enabling them to encounter their history in developmentally appropriate ways that will provide meaning to their lives as they come into their own. The Passover seder, in particular, the most celebrated Jewish holiday of the year,[37] is centered around passing on the "why" behind the traditions. Indeed, the arc of the evening is created by the youngest participant in the ritual asking the iconic question, Why is this night different from all other nights?[38]

For Generation Z and the Jewish experience, the question morphs, becoming, Why is this moment in history different from all other moments?

In 1965, renowned Jewish theologian Abraham Joshua Heschel posed the following conundrum to the General Assembly of the Council of Jewish Federation and Welfare Funds:

> Our young people are disturbed at parents who are spiritually insolvent. They seek direction, affirmation; they reject complacency and empty generosity. There is a waiting in many homes, in many hearts, for guidance, instruction, illumination, a waiting which is often intense, pressing, nationwide. So many are heartsick at the spiritual failure of our community. . . . To maintain devotion to Judaism, to succeed in the effort to convey my appreciation to my child, I need a community, as we all do. In this emergency, we call upon the Federation: Help us! Let us create an atmosphere of learning, a climate of reverence. . . . We must create a climate of elucidation, of pronouncing our people's waiting for meaning, by discovering and teaching the intellectual relevance of Judaism, by fostering reverence for learning and the learning of reverence.[39]

In many ways, the more things change, the more they stay the same. Concerns about how to engage young people are evergreen, like the sense that somehow, older generations are missing the mark and have somehow not yet figured out how to meaningfully reach the youngest members and emerging future leaders within the community. And at the same time, Jewish identity does seem to be at a watershed moment as Generation Z comes of age against an unprecedented historical backdrop.

Lila, a high school senior in Virginia, reflected on the moment that she truly understood what it meant to connect with her Jewish identity. "I was early one day for bat mitzvah practice. So I just sat in the synagogue, and I was all alone. I was just like—this is a holy moment. I hadn't experienced that before because I'm not religious. I want Judaism to be part of my life, and I talk about it a lot, even though I'm not involved with my synagogue anymore or the Jewish community as a whole, really. Being Jewish for me is a moral thing. It provides a backbone for the decisions that I make, and it makes me a stronger person."

In the final pages of *Jewish Pride*, Ben M. Freeman gives a resounding call to action: "Love our cultures and our traditions. Love our humour. Love our food. Love our diversity. Love our emphasis on learning and dialogue. Love our people. And, most of all, love our commitment to the continuation of Jewish life.[40] Jewish identity is complex and multifaceted. It confuses those who are Jewish and those who are not, because it cannot be succinctly defined. In the Talmud, the magnum opus of Jewish law and stories of rabbinic wisdom, the sage Hillel was challenged to explain the entire Torah to a prospective convert while the challenger stood on one foot. Hillel responded, "What is hateful to you, do not do to your neighbor. That is the whole Torah; the rest is the explanation of this—go and study it!"[41]

When it comes to the complexities of Jewish identity in the twenty-first century, there are many possible proverbial "on-one-foot" summaries:

Jewish identity means all of the things that make you realize you're part of something different and special because you're Jewish.

My Jewish identity makes me realize that I'm responsible to do something good and important in the world because of all of the things that my ancestors survived in order for me to be here.

Being Jewish for me is going to camp, being with friends, and lighting candles. And sometimes I'll be out at a store and I'll hear someone say something like "mazal tov," and I get excited even if I don't know them.

I'm not really sure what the most important thing about being Jewish is for me. But I know that it's something I'm proud of and I'm excited to pass it on to my kids if I ever have them.

I don't believe in God, or anything like that. But I always wear my Jewish star necklace because I believe in being proud of who I am, and who I am is Jewish.

Identity as a whole is at once a constant, as well as an ever-changing reality. In my practice as an educator, one of my core beliefs is that everything, even the getting-to-know-you games known as the icebreakers at the beginning of an encounter, are moments of pedagogy and opportunities to be taken seriously. A favorite icebreaker activity of mine is to have each participant make a list of the top ten nouns that define them and make them who they are in the world.

I'm a daughter.
I'm a brother.
I'm an athlete.
I'm a child of divorce.
I'm a friend.
I'm an artist.
I'm an activist.
I'm a barista.
I'm a student.
I'm a Jew.

After everyone makes their individual top-ten lists, they then have to go through the work—sometimes easy, sometimes soul-searchingly difficult work—of choosing which of the elements that make up who they are is the one that most sums them up. That's when the pushback comes: I can't pick just one thing! It depends! And then the choices are made, and the participants each announce what aspect of their overall complex, multifaceted identities is the one that tells everyone else everything they need to know about who they are. On the whole, the identifying element that's chosen is one that either is, or at least is perceived to be, lifelong. Barring extenuating, unforeseen events, I will always be a daughter. A sister. A Jew.

According to Martin Seligman, the originator of the school of thought known as positive psychology, the scientific study of what makes life most worth living, the theory of well-being can be summarized in the acronym PERMA: positive emotions, engagement, relationships, meaning, and accomplishment.[42] Each of the five elements is said to meet three criteria: they contribute to well-being, they are pursued for their own sake, and they can be defined and measured independently of the other elements. Each element is seen as important and valuable in the pursuit of a life of happiness and flourishing. As what it means to have a strong Jewish identity is continually reflected on and evaluated, finding the intersections of Jewish life and practice and flourishing can lead to moments of thriving.

Identity is determined by the individual in relation to the collective. When it comes to Jewish identity in particular, success at instilling it is an ever-changing target. The parent of several Generation Z–aged adolescents and emerging adults shared their perspective on what they hope Jewish identity will mean when their children set out on their own. "There's so much joy and so much to be excited about in Judaism. We want them to think Rosh Hodesh is great, and to be excited about *mishmar* learning on Thursday nights because that's when they get to eat *cholent* [an Eastern European hot dish]. There are so many opportunities to infuse life with joy, with celebrating, with helping people, with being part of a community, and bringing meals to people and making a *minyan* [prayer quorum]. There's a lot of good, and I want them to feel it."

Like the majority of the Generation Zers I spoke to, I have no memories of learning that Judaism is something that defines me. It's built into my DNA, courses through my blood, and pounds in my heart and head together with generations of memories, laughter, tears, and wisdom. I knew I was Jewish with my earliest words and felt it in my first steps. I do remember the first time I felt the need to hide my Judaism: at eighteen, on a plane, when the man sitting next to me asked what church I went to. And I remember the first time I felt othered as a Jew: as an adolescent, wondering why Christmas displays abounded while I couldn't find a Chanukah earring in any store. But most of all I remember the moments of pride. Standing with my arms linked around new friends on top of a mountain at sunrise. Organizing my first rally in support of Israel. Realizing that being part of the Jewish community means being able to create a home and a family wherever I go. Knowing that my identity links me to others around the world and throughout time and space. Not being able to explain it, or even particularly needing to, but holding it tight and letting it guide my steps. As one thought leader shared, when it comes to Jewish identity: "I hope that Jewishness will be a source of strength as Generation Z navigates the complexities of living in a complicated world. That it's something they can draw on, and feel has given them a grounding. I hope it makes them the best versions of themselves."

NOTES

1. Freeman, B. M. (2021). *Jewish pride: Rebuilding a people*. No Pasaran Media.

2. Erikson, E. (1968). *Identity: Youth and crisis*. New York: Norton.

3. Turner, J., & Oakes, P. (1986). "The significance of the social identity concept for social psychology with reference to individualism, interactionism and social influence." *British Journal of Social Psychology, 25*(3), 237–252.

4. Pew Research Center. (2013, October 1). A portrait of Jewish Americans. Chapter 3: Jewish identity. Retrieved from https://www.pewforum.org/2013/10/01/chapter-3-jewish-identity

5. Hanau, S. (2019, June 5). Jewish teens: "We don't want our parents' Judaism." *New York Jewish Week*. Retrieved from https://jewishweek.timesofisrael.com/jewish-teens-we-dont-want-our-parents-judaism

6. https://www.justice.gov/crt/fcs/TitleVI#

7. Schraub, D. (2019, December 12). Why Trump's executive order on anti-semitism touched off a firestorm. *The Atlantic*. Retrieved from https://www.theatlantic.com/ideas/archive/2019/12/dilemma-jewish-identity/603493

8. Kornbluh, J., & Weiss, M. (2019, December 11). A first look at the language of Trump's executive order on antisemitism. *Jewish Insider*. Retrieved from https://jewishinsider.com/2019/12/exclusive-a-first-look-at-the-language-of-trumps-executive-order-on-antisemitism

9. International Holocaust Remembrance Alliance (n.d.). Working definition of antisemitism. Retrieved from https://www.holocaustremembrance.com/working-definition-antisemitism

10. T'ruah (2019, December 11). Trump's executive order does nothing to protect Jews; Only restricts free speech. Retrieved from https://truah.org/press/truah-disturbed-by-executive-order-calling-judaism-a-nationality

11. French, S. E., Seidman, E., Allen, L., & Alber, J. L. (2006). The development of ethnic identity during adolescence. *Developmental Psychology, 42*(1), 1–10.

12. Ettinger, S. (n.d.). Jewish emancipation and enlightenment. My Jewish Learning. Retrieved from https://www.myjewishlearning.com/article/jewish-emancipation-and-enlightenment

13. Spokoiny, A. (2021, June 4). The Jews in the Pew: What the 2021 Pew report tells us about modern identity. *eJewishPhilanthropy*. Retrieved from https://ejewishphilanthropy.com/the-jews-in-the-pew-what-the-2021-pew-report-tells-us-about-modern-identity

14. How we gather. https://caspertk.files.wordpress.com/2015/04/how -we-gather.pdf

15. Desjardins, J. (2019, February 14). Meet Generation Z: The newest member to the workforce. *Visual Capitalist*. Retrieved from https://www .visualcapitalist.com/meet-generation-z-the-newest-member-to-the-work force

16. Young, L. (2019, October 2). Gen Z is the most progressive—and least partisan—generation. *Teen Vogue*. Retrieved from https://www.teen vogue.com/story/how-will-gen-z-vote

17. Munsey, C. (2006). Emerging adults: The in-between age. *Monitor, 37*(7). Retrieved from https://www.apa.org/monitor/jun06/emerging

18. Shlain, T. (2019, October 1). Everything you need to enjoy one tech-free day a week. *Wired*. Retrieved from https://www.wired.com/story /everything-you-need-to-enjoy-one-tech-free-day-a-week

19. Leviticus 11:7–8.

20. Exodus 23:19.

21. Tractate Hullin 8:4.

22. Yanklowitz, S. (n.d.). What is "ethical" kashrut? My Jewish Learning. Retrieved from https://www.myjewishlearning.com/article/ethical-kashrut

23. https://theculturetrip.com/middle-east/israel/articles/how-shakshuka -israels-famous-breakfast-dish-took-the-world-by-storm

24. Twitty, M. (n.d.). Kosher soul Shabbat. *Afroculinaria*.

25. Fischler, C. (1988). Food, self and identity. *Social Science Information, 27*, 275–293. Retrieved from https://oglethorpe.edu/wp-content /uploads/2020/01/food-self-identity.pdf

26. Kraut, A. M. (2004). Ethnic foodways: The significance of food in the designation of cultural boundaries between immigrant groups in the U.S., 1840–1921. *Journal of American Jewish Culture, 2*(3), 409–420.

27. Moss, A. (n.d.) Why no flowers on Jewish graves? Chabad. Retrieved from https://www.chabad.org/library/article_cdo/aid/1911395/jewish/Why -No-Flowers-on-Jewish-Graves.htm

28. Salkin, A. (2009, May 22). American Girl's journey to the Lower East Side. *New York Times*. Retrieved from https://www.nytimes.com /2009/05/24/fashion/24Doll.html

29. Schneider, E. (2018, December 3). I re-read American Girl's Rebecca Rubin books, and they hold up. *Jewish Book Council*. Retrieved from https://www.jewishbookcouncil.org/pb-daily/i-re-read-the-american -girl-rebecca-rubin-books

30. Rose, O. N., Green Kaiser, J. E., & Klein, M. (2008). *Righteous indignation: A Jewish call for justice.* Nashville, TN: Jewish Lights Publishing, p. 22.

31. Blidstein, G. J. (1997). Tikkun olam. In D. Shatz, C. I. Waxman, and N. J. Diament (Eds.), *Tikkun olam: Social responsibility in Jewish thought and law* (pp. 17–60). Northvale, NJ: Jason Aronson.

32. My Jewish Learning. (n.d.). Tikkun olam: Repairing the world. Retrieved from https://www.myjewishlearning.com/article/tikkun-olam -repairing-the-world

33. Alper, B. A., & Cooperman, A. (2021, May 11). 10 key findings about Jewish Americans. Pew Research Center. Retrieved from https:// www.pewresearch.org/fact-tank/2021/05/11/10-key-findings-about -jewish-americans

34. Collins, C. (2018). What is white privilege, really? *Learning for Justice, 60.* Retrieved from https://www.learningforjustice.org/magazine/fall -2018/what-is-white-privilege-really

35. Yama, L. (2021, April 6). Dispelling the model minority myth must include Jewish Americans. *Washington Square News.* Retrieved from https://nyunews.com/opinion/2021/04/06/activism-must-include-jewish -americans

36. Margot, J. S. (2020). *Mazel tov: The story of my extraordinary friendship with an Orthodox Jewish family.* London: Pushkin Press.

37. Markoe, L. (2016, April 22). Passover, most beloved Jewish holiday, explained. *USA* Today. Retrieved from https://www.usatoday.com/story /news/world/2016/04/22/passover-jewish-holiday-explained/83387514

38. My Jewish Learning. (n.d.). The Four Questions. Retrieved from https://www.myjewishlearning.com/article/the-four-questions

39. Shrage, B. (2009). "Abraham Joshua Heschel and the creation of the Jewish Renaissance." *Modern Judaism*, *29*(1), pp. 58–61.

40. Freeman, *Jewish pride.*

41. Babylonian Talmud, Shabbat 31a.

42. Sze, D. (2015, June 17). The father of positive psychology and his two theories of happiness. HuffPost.

TEN

Where Do We Go from Here?

A Jew is asked to take a leap of action, rather than a leap of faith.
—Rabbi Abraham Joshua Heschel

Throughout the writing of this book, I found myself struggling to find the endpoint. Like the Generation Zers I spoke to, nearly every day I would wind up "doom scrolling," unable to tear myself away from the latest crisis du jour making headlines in the news and on social media. The increasing bifurcation of American society across ideological boundaries disturbed me, as it became harder to figure out who my allies could be in fighting antisemitism. Amanda Berman from Zioness validated this concern. "Antisemitism from the Left and the Right is actually very similar. Antisemitism in general manifests as conspiracy theories." This all came to a head on January 6, 2021. The insurrection at the U.S. Capitol brought the undercurrent of antisemitism to the seat of power of the United States and shed light on the disconnect between how the Jewish community sees threats against it and how the rest of the world accepts this status quo. In Jewish circles and among Jewish friends, the threats against us in particular, as well as the collective of American democracy, were obviously apparent. Seeing infiltrators proudly wearing clothing with insignias including Camp Auschwitz and 6MWNE (6 Million Were Not Enough) was chilling. But the silence was even colder. Zeke, the high school student from Maryland we heard from earlier, summarized the desire for words of support, particularly from the top. "We need the government saying antisemitism isn't tolerated. They can say we don't tolerate hate or violence, but specifically this type of hate isn't called out. I want leaders to say, 'We don't tolerate racism *and* we don't tolerate antisemitism.'"

Instead, many Jews experienced a sense of isolation, coming to terms with the lack of an outcry. While the insurrection itself was widely derided, the dangerously churning undercurrent of antisemitism was not a headline topic. For Generation Zers trying to reconcile their Judaism and their Americanism, this discrepancy could not be ignored. "Our generation is definitely an activist generation. We're being raised to speak our voices, so we're not going to stand down when we see blatant antisemitism. We're going to fight it." Zeke, the Maryland-based high schooler we've heard from throughout, is echoed in his words by Elisheva, the Jewish/Romani Instagrammer, who concurs about the power of Generation Z when it comes to speaking out and acting. "If you're going to call us snowflakes,[1] keep in mind that we can cause accidents on the road. We're a damn force to be reckoned with. People say we're too sensitive, but really we're displaying empathy and compassion for others."

Lisa, in the context of speaking about her work in the field of Holocaust education, noted that when examining the past, "It's important to understand what happened. But it's also important to see both the perpetrators and the bystanders as human beings. Each one of us is capable of great harm. So how will we make choices differently?" At this moment in history, we are in close proximity to a rapidly unfolding and seemingly constantly changing series of events that challenge assumptions and preconceived notions about the world as we know it. Without the benefit of historical context and the ability to look back and analyze contemporary events thoughtfully, we are left engaging with our circumstances as a moving target. Taking the lessons of history and the complexities of the present, one can come away with equally compelling worldviews. Are the Jewish people meant to internalize the knowledge that the tragedies of history and of today demonstrate a need to look inward toward self-defense, as others are out to get us? Or should we feel a broader sense of obligation, looking beyond the porous boundaries of the Jewish community to be allies and champions of others?

Over the course of less than two weeks in May 2021, the United States saw an increase in antisemitic incidents, many directly related to Operation Guardian of the Walls, a fifteen-day flare-up of the Israeli-Palestinian conflict.[2] As Israeli population centers were barraged by Hamas rockets, and the Israeli army targeted weapons caches in the Gaza Strip, the fallout from the increased tensions reached cities and smartphones around the world. Over the course of just over a week, the Anti-Defamation League reported receiving nearly 200 reports of antisemitic incidents, up from 131 the week before the conflict began, including hate crimes, physical attacks, and online slurs.[3] During the period from May 7 to May 14, 2021, the days immediately following the start of the violence, an analysis of Twitter saw over 17,000 tweets that used variations of the phrase "Hitler was right."[4]

For Generation Zers, particularly those who have worked to be allies to other minority communities in their times of need, the antisemitic sentiments, coupled with the silence of friends, celebrities, and leaders, have echoed loudly. Alyssa Weinstein-Sears, the Houston-based Holocaust educator we met in chapter 2, gave insights on the experience of silence from those whom one would have expected or hoped to be allies. "You can't speak out against racism and be antisemitic and vice versa. If you're being anti-racist, you also need to be antihatred of Jewish people." Despite this, however, many Generation Zers have been hurt and disturbed by the silence they've seen, particularly on social media.

"I think I've unfollowed 30 people on Instagram this week. These are people who I used to look up to, and who I love seeing their pictures. But seeing their one-sidedness and the antisemitism they're sharing in their posts, I can't continue. It's becoming a mental health drain for me." Jill, an Ohio-based teen, shared that her social media feed has become a battleground. "I'll see the news about all these attacks,[5] but then instead of calling it out, it's almost like all these people are saying the Jews deserve it. I'm scared—it's like, do they think that about me too?"

With the uptick in antisemitism, new choices are being made with regard to what it means to be publicly Jewish. The presence of ritual objects on homes and bodies have come to feel like targets for some,[6] while others have had a spirit of defiance, displaying Stars of David, Israeli flags, and changing their social media profiles to blue in solidarity. Ultimately, however, systemic changes will need to happen now that there's an increased awareness of how easy it is for an undercurrent of antisemitism to boil over. According to the 2020 Pew research conducted on the American Jewish community, which came out only days before the start of Operation Guardian of the Walls, more than half of American Jews reported feeling less safe as a result of their perceptions of antisemitism than they did five years ago, with 61 percent of "visible Jews" reporting this increased sense of lack of safety.[7]

In reflecting on ways to intentionally counter the increase in antisemitism, Blythe, a Barnard college student, wrote in an article in October

2020, "Education on religion, especially religious minorities, must be an imperative core study. Identities beyond the privileged majority have too long been treated like elective material. Students need to be forced to look beyond themselves to attain a global perspective that will serve them long-term. I do not think students choose to be unaware of the beliefs around them, but they have simply never been expected to know or have the courtesy of understanding religious differences as it has not been a prioritized teaching."[8]

Jess, the New Jersey–based social worker and descendant of Holocaust survivors, shared how the legacy of her familial experience impacts the Jewish experience of the twenty-first century. "It could easily happen again. All you need is someone in power, with followers, and something horrible could easily happen. So we need to look out for each other." Deborah Fripp, the Holocaust storytelling educator from Texas, noted what makes this historical juncture different from the years leading up to the Holocaust from her perspective. This time around, "we [the Jewish people] are not helpless. There are things we can do to stop it. [The shooting in] Pittsburgh was not *Kristallnacht*.[9] This time, the police are on *our* side."

Dina from Maryland, a mother of two Generation Zers, disagreed with Deborah's assessment of how authority figures and institutions factor into antisemitism in the United States at this juncture. From her perspective, "coming out of the Trump era, it's OK to be an antisemite. And it's OK to be out and proud as an antisemite. Whether or not they've always been there, to have people as out and proud antisemites is scary. And somehow there's been this pairing of patriotism and antisemitism. It's so much more 'in your face' than it's ever been before."

Amanda Berman noted her lack of astonishment at the current status quo. "As our society has been deconstructed during the Trump administration, it's not surprising that antisemitism has been on the rise." However, Amanda is not blaming either the Left or the Right exclusively for the uptick in antisemitism that the Jewish community has experienced. "The shooting at the Jersey City kosher grocery store was *not* a neo-Nazi.[10] This is not all a white supremacist threat. I reject the notion that the only physical threat is from the Right and that Jews are otherwise safe to express their identities. Of course, this isn't appreciated by people who would rather politicize this issue."

Alyssa Weinstein-Sears gave her insights on antisemitism's newest face. "Antisemitism today is a new brand. It's a post-Holocaust brand of antisemitism. So if you want to make a splash, just post some swastikas on a cemetery and you can be famous. There's a piece of it that wants attention and recognition. But at the end of the day, this isn't a new hatred. Everyone needs someone to blame, and the cliché is to blame the Jews. I hear people saying antisemitic things all the time, and they don't even know any Jewish people. It's dehumanization. And it's classic."

Hannah echoed Alyssa: "There's an issue right now with people in power. There's this obsession with who has power, and who's exploiting it. There's a wave of Far-Left antisemitism that says the Zionists have it. And then the Far Right says the Jews have it. They're both really talking about the same people. So people need to know that antisemitism is alive and well and mutates with the current culture."

When I spoke with Mara, the SUNY Binghamton freshman, she shared that her biggest challenge with Judaism is the idea of Amalek. "The idea that there's this unredeemable people that will always be bad is just very out of line with the rest of Judaism for me." In chapter 2, we explored Amalek in relation to the legacy of the Holocaust. But for Mara, the idea of Amalek, the traditional enemy of the Jewish people, felt disingenuous with the Jewish values she had been raised with. And indeed, redemption and forgiveness are part of the social justice–based Judaism that many Generation Zers have been raised on. The challenge then becomes, How does that liberal, progressive worldview intersect with raw manifestations of hatred?

Alicia, the mother of two Generation Zers in Los Angeles, shared her dilemma in this regard. "I don't want them to be so sheltered that when [antisemitism] comes up, they're so flabbergasted that they don't know what to do. I also don't want the world to be scary, but at the same time, I want them to know that this is there, and it's real. How do you differentiate between moments for conversation and moments that are just wrong?" While the burden of antisemitism should not rest on the collective shoulders of the Jewish community, it is Jews who are on the front lines of responding to its resurgence. Alicia continued, "There are opportunities to lean in and times when apologies can happen, rather than enacting cancel culture. But then there are things that are antisemitic and unacceptable. I want them to take the opportunity to have conversations, but sometimes things are wrong and you just need to call them out."

For Generation Z, the dilemma between calling *out* and calling *in* is a complicated one. Generation Zers, as we have seen, are known for being a tolerant and accepting demographic cohort. They have strong beliefs but also want to be accepting and to create space for a plurality of individuals. Bailey noted that from her perspective, "the worst thing you can do is compare pain and suffering. It's best to step back from a comparative stance and to do what you can for whoever is suffering, rather than using one to invalidate the other."

When it comes to the complexities of contemporary society, particularly as it relates to identity politics, there is a tremendous amount of work to be done regarding finding the intersections between Jewish values and the conversations happening throughout the United States and the world. Young Jews are inclined to look at things through a critical lens and can easily spot the gaps in what is being presented to them. As Lily, who works with Generation Zers, shared, "When our values come into conflict with one another, that's the hardest thing. Generation Zers are capable of holding onto multiple truths at the same time, but when they contradict each other, ultimately, they'll have to make a choice. Our hope is that the choices that they make lead them to find value in the way we've taught them, but in the end we can't know for sure."

In the Jewish liturgical tradition, every week of the year there is a designated Torah portion—a selection of biblical readings that are publicly recited, privately read, and collectively pored over around the world. The order of readings never changes, and indeed, on Simchat Torah, the holiday that celebrates the conclusion of the annual cycle of readings, a point is made to read the first verses once again, starting the cycle over immediately. For many, this inexhaustible routine can feel daunting or frustrating or even meaningless. Is there any other text that would be read over and over again, without ceasing? In Pirkei Avot, the Ethics of the Fathers, on the topic of the Torah, it is written, "Ben Bag-Bag used to say: Turn it and turn it again, for everything is in it. Pore over it, and wax gray and old over it. Stir not from it, for you can have no better rule than it."[11] Each year, as the Jewish people return to the same texts again and again, the words themselves never change. But who we are changes, and the way that we approach the text, bringing our lived experiences, new knowledge, feelings, and all the elements of who we are, is always different. Words that may make no sense one year are the most poignant the next.

When we look at antisemitism, in many ways we're once again facing the same problems that we've seen every year, in every generation. It's we who are different. Generation Z comes to age-old dilemmas with fresh eyes, new perspectives, and an understanding of the world that is unique to its moment in history. In the most iconic words from the classic book *A Tale of Two Cities*, Charles Dickens wrote, "It was the best of times, it was the worst of times." At this juncture in Jewish and world history, we can hold multiple truths. There has never been a better time to be Jewish. Never have there been more opportunities, more ways to express oneself, more spaces that are accepting, welcoming, and embracing of who the Jewish people are. Never have the Jewish people had the confidence that comes with having power and authority. Never has there been a generation, like Generation Z, that has unfettered access, unlimited potential for growth and reach, and spaces to create change literally at their fingertips.

At the same time, with the generation of Holocaust survivors nearing their collective end, never before has there been less certainty about the future of the Jewish people and the legacy of their story. Indisputable historical facts are seen as questionable, and conspiracy theories that feel more at home in propaganda from the former Soviet Union are being shared in the halls of power, in the echo chambers of the internet, and in social circles of every demographic. While antisemitism has never gone away, and in many ways this chapter of human history is simply the continuation of an eternal story, in others it feels different and needs to be addressed as such.

Antisemitism on the Right brings up practical and physical concerns about safety for many Jewish Generation Zers. From the Left, there's something else—an intellectual and emotional fear that stifles engagement and discourse. The polarization of society places Generation Zers into a space of feeling the need to choose between the two, and it is an act of bravery and self-determination to carve out an individual path that allows for rigorous exploration of the self, the collective, and the truth. Standing up to antisemitism is seen by some as obligatory, by others as heroic, and by still others as burdensome. Regardless of how each Generation Zer responds, the reality of hate as a component of the Jewish experience is shared. And in a world that forces Jewish adolescents and emerging adults to view their heritage at least in part through a lens of victimhood, it becomes even more of a challenge for them to focus on growing, living, and thriving.

As a Jewish educator, people have lots of guesses about what the hardest and best parts of my job must be. Among the elements that others consider to be top contenders for the hardest, there's recruiting participants from an overprogrammed population, dealing with the sometimes-conflicting demands of parents and learners, never having enough time, and limited resources. All true. Likewise, some of the top guesses about the best parts are making an impact on young people, constantly learning new things, participating in immersive experiences, and being able to align my passions, values, and profession. Again, all true. But the at once hardest and best part of my job is being an authentic Jewish personality, a role model, with flaws and questions and ingrained truths that my learners can relate to, be challenged by, and learn from.

For those who are coming of age during the resurgence of hate, and those who care about them, allowing for the gray area, that between the black and white of right and wrong, to be a place of meaning making will be critical. So, too, will be finding the authentic truths that guide them in their life journeys. As for where that leaves the status quo with regard to antisemitism, the story will continue to unfold.

In a previous moment of destruction for the Jewish people, the destruction of the Temple in Jerusalem, Rabbi Yochanan ben Zakkai arranged for his students to fake his own death and smuggle him out of the city in a coffin. The coffin was carried to the tent of the Roman general, Vespasian. Yochanan ben Zakkai revealed himself to Vespasian and pleaded with the general for a place to be set aside where he could start a new school and study Torah in peace. This new place, known as Yavne, became the new center of Jewish learning after the destruction of the Temple. Yochanan ben Zakkai effectively saved Jewish education and collective wisdom to be reenvisioned by a new generation, ushering in the age of rabbinic Judaism.[12] But while his results were tremendous, they were not without controversy. Was this leader right to abandon the fighting, dying populace in search of greener pastures? If he had had the opportunity to negotiate with the enemy, should he have used it to save the Temple instead of giving in to its inevitable defeat and looking for a plan B?

Yochanan ben Zakkai was a realist, a pragmatist, and a dreamer. His actions allowed for Judaism to survive, adapting to a new world order and creating continuity and innovation out of destruction. At this moment, when the world seems to be at a new precipice point, who are the ben Zakkais, negotiating for a new future?

Antisemitism is in many ways inevitable. There is no history without it, no civilization that has not victimized the Jews either physically or in effigy. But Generation Z's lesson for the world is that there is no status quo that is irreversible. They are rewriting history, seeking to turn back the clock on climate change, and calling into question countless elements of society that were previously thought to be the inevitable "way things are." With the right encouragement and opportunity, this can be the time when antisemitism is given its own platform to be acknowledged for the destruction it brings to whole civilizations and to be dealt with accordingly.

If you're a Generation Zer, a Jew, an ally, or an interested learner, the message that I leave you with is this: for the Jewish people, time is not linear. There is no past to be left behind, nor is there ever a stable present or an inevitable future. The past is with us, with the hard-won knowledge of what can happen when hatred is allowed to flow unchecked and even encouraged. The future is ours to make. And the present is the confluence of the two, informed by history and memory and dreams of what can be. Antisemitism, in many ways, is the through line—challenging us to answer the call of history to create the future.

NOTES

1. McKay, R. (2020, February 24). Who are snowflakes: Generation snowflake and the controversial word. *New Idea*. Retrieved from https://www.newidea.com.au/snowflake-generation

2. Katz, Y. (2021, May 21). Israel's Gaza war is like no other military operation in history—opinion. *Jerusalem Post*. Retrieved from https://www.jpost.com/opinion/israels-gaza-operation-is-like-no-other-military-op-in-history-opinion-668709

3. McEvoy, J. (2021, May 20). Synagogue attacks and slurs: Jewish community rocked by rise in anti-semitism amid Israel-Gaza fighting. *Forbes*. Retrieved from https://www.forbes.com/sites/jemimamcevoy/2021/05/20/synagogue-attacks-and-slurs-jewish-community-rocked-by-rise-in-anti-semitism-amid-israel-gaza-fighting

4. Anti-Defamation League (2021, May 20). Preliminary ADL data reveals uptick in antisemitic incidents linked to recent Mideast violence. Retrieved from https://www.adl.org/news/press-releases/preliminary-adl-data-reveals-uptick-in-antisemitic-incidents-linked-to-recent

5. Hanau, S., Sales, B., & Kampeas, R. (2021, May 22). As Gaza conflict triggers antisemitism, some US Jews hide religious symbols. *Times of Israel*. Retrieved from https://www.timesofisrael.com/israel-gaza-conflict-has-triggered-a-wave-of-antisemitic-incidents-in-us

6. Hanau, S., & Sales, B. (2021, May 21). Some American Jews are taking off their kippahs and Stars of David amid a wave of antisemitic incidents. *Jewish Telegraphic Agency*. Retrieved from https://www.jta.org/2021/05/21/united-states/the-israel-gaza-conflict-triggered-a-wave-of-antisemitic-incidents-some-american-jews-are-taking-off-their-kippahs-and-stars-of-david

7. Rosenfeld, A. (2021, May 12). Pew's new study of American Jews reveals widening divides, worries over antisemitism. *Jewish Boston*. Retrieved from https://www.jewishboston.com/read/pews-new-study-of -american-jews-reveals-widening-divides-worries-over-antisemitism

8. Drucker, B. (2020, October 21). To fight antisemitism, all schools need to teach about Judaism. *Alma*. Retrieved from https://www.heyalma .com/to-fight-antisemitism-all-schools-need-to-teach-about-judaism

9. Berenbaum, M. (2018, December 20). Kristallnacht. *Encyclopædia Britannica*.

10. Hanna, J., & Holcombe, M. (2019, December 12). Jersey City shoot-ers fueled by hatred of Jewish people and law enforcement, state attorney general says. CNN. Retrieved from https://edition.cnn.com/2019/12/12/us /jersey-city-new-jersey-shooting-thursday

11. Pirkei Avot 5:26.

12. Yochanan ben Zakkai. *Jewish Virtual Library*.

APPENDIX A

Learning Guide for Jewish Communities

This book is meant to be the start of conversations, of reflections, and of reckonings for individuals and communities. As a Jewish educator, I believe in the importance of being in dialogue with a text. This book is a jumping-off point, with each voice highlighted within as its own series of vignettes ready to be studied, unpacked, and put in relationship with your own lived experiences and those of your community. The classic Jewish learning methodology of *hevruta* brings together seekers of knowledge as peers, encountering the text on equal terms and responding to it. I hope that this text will be read by individuals, as well as in hevruta, and that however you're approaching it as a reader and a learner, you'll embrace the multidirectional relationship that is core to experiential education.

The content of this book is challenging. It's hard to grapple with the unknowns of an ever-changing world, particularly coming out of an unprecedented global pandemic. Generation Zers are inheriting a world of polarization, complexity, and hard choices. This is true in the global context in general but is particularly true within Jewish communal spaces. The 2020 Pew Report on the American Jewish community, among its other key data pieces, found that 40 percent of Jewish adults ages eighteen to twenty-nine don't identify with religion. At the same time, 17 percent of individuals in that same age bracket identify as Orthodox. "In other words, [young adult] U.S. Jews count among their ranks both a relatively large share of traditionally observant, Orthodox Jews and an even larger group of people who see themselves as Jewish for cultural, ethnic or family reasons but do not identify with Judaism—as a religion—at all."[1]

This dichotomy, wherein there is an increasing polarization in the Jewish community, is not necessarily a surprising statistic, but it is one to be mindful of. With antisemitism on the rise, coupled with growing divisions in the Jewish community, it's easy to worry about becoming fragmented as a community. Some of us don't always feel that the rest of the Jewish community is in solidarity with us—and some of us may feel like things are so polarized that we aren't even part of the same community at this point. It may feel like there's more that divides us than unites us. I say this not to minimize anyone's feelings but rather to acknowledge that in many ways, there isn't a single Jewish community to unite behind. Generation Zers, like millennials, are proponents of unbundling. Rather than relying on one organization, space, or group for everything—from personal support to life-cycle events, recreation to a sense of fulfillment—they are more likely to choose to affiliate differently for different stages, needs, and occasions. Perhaps one Jewish community cannot reasonably be thought of as capable of meaningfully meeting that multitude of needs.

But at the same time, the multiple on-ramps to connecting with Jewish community and your own Jewish identity hopefully mean that wherever you are and whatever you're seeking, there is a place for you. And my hope is that this book can be a small part of that journey. If you've read it alone, find someone—in your in-person community, online, Jewish or not—to unpack it with. Pose a question or pick a topic that challenged or surprised you, and present it to your thought partner. While you may not have all the answers, they may not have all the answers, and the text itself by no means has all of the exhaustive answers. The triangulated conversations that will surely ensue will bring up more questions, more answers, and more insights than any of us can hope to achieve alone.

When reading this book as individuals and as a Jewish community, I encourage you to explore it through the lens of the following questions:

1. *Regardless of your demographic within the overall Jewish community, the unfortunate odds are that you or someone you know has experienced overt or subtle antisemitism. This may be uncomfortable to admit—it's hard to acknowledge having been a victim of hatred, and in a period in world history when so many other minority groups are also being systemically victimized, it may feel like antisemitic*

microaggressions are "first-world problems." But the oppression Olympics is a game that has no winners, and all experiences of hate are legitimate and painful. **Is antisemitism a part of your Jewish story? Is it something you acknowledge or actively think about? Does antisemitism, or the fear of it, play a role in the Jewish choices that you make?**

2. *Too often, many Generation Zers are encouraged to tap into connecting with the Jewish community and their own Jewish identities when antisemitism rears its head, because well-meaning parents and grandparents are concerned about the well-being of the next generation of the Jewish people. This concern is deeply legitimate. But if someone's Jewish identity becomes important solely because of the hate it may manifest for others, it ceases to be a value-add in and of itself. In* Jewish Pride, *Ben M. Freeman wrote, "Love our cultures and our traditions. Love our humour. Love our food. Love our diversity. Love our emphasis on learning and dialogue. Love our people. And, most of all, love our commitment to the continuation of Jewish life."* **What do you love about being Jewish? What inspires you in your Judaism? What is the value that you find in your Jewish identity and experiences?**

3. *The Holocaust is the most iconic, tragic, unthinkable manifestation of antisemitism in history. In many ways, it has irrevocably impacted the collective psyche of the Jewish people, as well as the mentality of each individual Jew, regardless of whether they are descendants of survivors. For many, it has manifested in one of two ways. For some, the Holocaust has triggered a survival instinct, a sense that the world is full of those who are out to get the Jews, that manifests in looking inward and focusing on Jewish continuity above all else. For others, understanding that our collective ancestors have experienced such an inhumane tragedy has inspired an external worldview, emphasizing allyship and helping whomever is in a vulnerable position, because we know what it's like to be the ones in need of help.* **What drives you in your actions? Is there a mindset that you align with more than the other? Is it something that's easy for you to admit, even to yourself?**

4. *In the United States of 2021, as well as around the world, there is no shortage of manifestations of antisemitism. We see it increasing on the political Left and the Right, on social media, in person, from*

authority figures, related to Israel, and even from members of the Jewish community directed toward those who are not like them. The challenge that comes with having so many iterations of antisemitism is that it becomes very easy to point fingers, focusing on the problems that align with our overall worldviews—the Left calling out the Right and vice versa. But being able to look externally often prevents us from doing the soul-searching work of looking internally at the problems within our own camps and not treating the root causes of the uptick in antisemitism around the world. **If you take a hard look at your own spaces, politically, religiously, and otherwise, do you see antisemitism? What are the steps you can take toward addressing it?**

5. *Whether you're a member of Generation Z or are interested in how the experiences of Generation Z are both indicative of and shaping the world that all of us are living in, Generation Z's reality impacts all of us. It will shape workplaces, religious institutions, governments, systems of belief, and countless aspects, large and small, of how we live our lives. In an increasingly diverse world, an increasingly connected world, and an increasingly polarized world, multiple realities can exist at once.* **How do you think Generation Z's experience of Jewish identity, and of antisemitism, is unique? How is it part of the ongoing story of the Jewish people?**

NOTE

1. Mirsky, M. (2021, May 11). New Pew study of American Jews: Deep questions, surprising answers. *JWeekly.* Retrieved from https://www.jweekly.com/2021/05/11/new-pew-study-of-american-jews-deep-questions-surprising-answers

APPENDIX B

Learning Guide for Allies

To the educators, allies, and other non-Jewish readers who have picked up and read this book: thank you. Your role in all of this is critical and cannot be overstated. Earlier in this book, I quoted Rabbi Lord Jonathan Sacks, the late former chief rabbi of the United Kingdom, and I think his words are important enough that they merit being repeated here: antisemitism is not a Jewish problem. It is a problem that has been projected onto Jews. As allies in the work to combat antisemitism, you are critical partners in the ultimate betterment of society. Throughout history, as we know, antisemitism has too often been the warning bell ringing to alert us of systemic problems, intolerance, and hate threatening the entire community. But it's up to all of us to listen, to know the warning signs, and to take the steps to counter them, rather than brushing them aside. By educating yourself, you have taken a critical first step along the path of allyship, and it shouldn't be understated how important that is.

Your role as an ally is often a challenging one. Antisemitism is a tricky form of discrimination. As the world's oldest hatred, we would think that it would be overt and easy to recognize. After all, we see in the news when antisemitism indisputably bubbles over. Headstones in Jewish cemeteries are defaced and toppled over, visibly Jewish-looking people are more likely to be victims of assault, and noticeably Jewish spaces are targeted with threats of violence. We know what to do in these scenarios. We issue statements of solidarity and support, decry the latest manifestation of this ancient hate, and promise ourselves that Never Again still stands—we would *never* let things escalate that far. Surely we would notice before anything got too bad, and our society wouldn't allow it anyway.

Being a bystander is an active choice. As we saw throughout this book, it's the subtle things that we let slip under the threshold of social norms that permeate our collective psyche, rather than outlying shock and awe events. It's the fear of a complex unknown that many non-Jewish would-be allies are silenced by. The experiences like the Society of Children's Book Writers and Illustrators had when they issued a statement condemning antisemitism in June 2021, and then, a mere seventeen days later, had to walk it back due to an outcry. The original statement said:

> The SCBWI unequivocally recognizes that the world's 14.7 million Jewish people (less than 0.018% of the population) have the right to life, safety, and freedom from scapegoating and fear. No person should be at risk because of their heritage, religion, disability, or whom they love…Because antisemitism is one of the oldest forms of hatred, it has its own name. It is the example from which many forms of racism and violence are perpetuated…it saddens us that for the 4th time this year, we are compelled to invite you to join us in not looking away and in speaking out against all forms of hate, including antisemitism.[1]

In the subsequent letter, SCBWI executive director Lin Oliver wrote, "I would like to apologize to everyone in the Palestinian community who felt unrepresented, silenced, or marginalized. SCBWI acknowledges the pain our actions have caused to our Palestinian and Muslim members."[2]

Though the original statement did not mention Israel, the condemnation of antisemitism unequivocally somehow triggered members of SCBWI. But I encourage you, as an ally and a learner, to take a step back. How does this compare to saying "All lives matter" in response to the Black Lives Matter movement? If someone finds themselves bristling against the erasure of BIPOC pain when someone says all lives matter, but are not concerned when antisemitism is not allowed to be condemned on its own terms, it can and should bring up some uncomfortable questions. Why does it bother me? Do I not see Jews as minorities in need of allyship? If I replaced the words Jew and antisemitism with any other minority group and the hatred directed toward them, would I feel the same way?

The subtleties of antisemitism—erasure, gaslighting, and minimizing legitimate pain—are often the most concerning, particularly for Generation Zers. For Jewish Generation Z, seeing themselves as victims is not a desired state of being, nor is it one that comes naturally. Generation Zers are proud of all that they are, with all of the messiness that comes with being intersectional, multifaceted individuals. So where does that leave us, and particularly you—the allies and partners in creating the future that all of us are striving toward?

SEEK OUT OPPORTUNITIES TO CONNECT WITH THE JEWISH COMMUNITY

Though the Jewish community in the United States is less than 2 percent of the overall population, there is no shortage of Jews (in every state, and online) who are ready to meet with you, talk to you, and learn with you. By connecting with the Jewish community, you'll put faces to the amorphous people described on the news or in books. Reach out to individuals or community organizations that interest you and find ways to get involved. Ask questions, read, and you're sure to find an entry point to connecting with the Jewish community in a way that's meaningful to you.

EXTEND MESSAGES OF SUPPORT IF/WHEN ANTISEMITISM BECOMES AN ISSUE, WHEREVER YOU ARE AND WHATEVER IT LOOKS LIKE

When antisemitism rears its head, part of what makes it so isolating for the Jewish community is the sense of being alone, against the world, without partners sharing in the righteous indignation of discrimination. As an informed ally, you can make an immeasurably positive impact by reaching out and letting those in your local and extended Jewish communities know that you feel their collective pain and share in it. Even more so, as appropriate, you can share on social media, raising awareness about experiences of antisemitism and sharing within your own community and network how these acts are unacceptable. Your commitment and setting an example of outspoken partnership, both out loud and behind the scenes, send the message that the Jewish community is not alone and that fighting antisemitism is not just "a Jewish problem."

LISTEN TO YOUR JEWISH FRIENDS AND PEERS. IF THEY SAY SOMETHING COUNTS AS ANTISEMITISM, BELIEVE THEM IN THEIR DISCOMFORT

Just as when other forms of discrimination are noted by their victims, such as an LGBTQ+ person pointing out microaggressions that manifest as homophobia or a BIPOC individual highlighting what actions, either intentionally or unintentionally, qualify as racism, when Jewish individuals point to something as antisemitism, they are correct in identifying their lived experiences. In many instances, when members of the Jewish community call something out as antisemitism, rather than being met with sympathy and support, their experiences are questioned and debated by others. Questions are asked as to whether or not something "counts" as antisemitism, or if the intent is what matters as opposed to how the words or actions are received. As an ally, just as you would be to any other minority group, allow the Jewish community, and the victims of antisemitism, to take the lead in naming it. Believe someone when they say they experienced antisemitism, and support them as you would any other minority who is a victim and survivor of hate.

INCLUDE JEWS IN YOUR DEFINITIONS OF DIVERSITY AND INCLUSION

Too often, because of the stereotypes we've shared throughout this book, including that Jews are generally assumed to be both white and privileged, Jews are not viewed through the same lens as other minority groups. While the lived experiences of the Jewish community collectively are not necessarily the same as any other group's when it comes to issues of diversity and inclusion, the Jewish community needs to be on society's collective radar. As recently as 2021, six campuses within the University of Wisconsin system made the decision to begin classes on Rosh Hashanah, the Jewish new year and one of the most sacred days on the Jewish calendar. Despite pushback and protests from students, alumni, and professors, the administration stuck to a decision that would systematically set an unwelcoming tone for the campus Jewish community. This one example is part of a larger story augmented by many others, wherein the needs of Jews as a distinct minority population are not taken into account, even in spaces with many Jews and even where there is an overall commitment to inclusion. Be a change in those spaces—question how the Jewish calendar, or Jewish dietary restrictions, are being taken into account when planning for an inclusive environment.

NOTES

1. #StopAntisemitism: A statement from SCBWI.
2. Deutch, G. (2021, July 2). The battle raging over antisemitism and Israel in the kids' literature world. *Jewish Insider.* Retrieved from https://jewishinsider.com/2021/07/antisemitism-israel-kids-literature

Index

Adolescence, 6–7, 40, 112, 115, 123, 126
    identity development, 6–7, 123
    parental relationships, 112
    peer groups, 7, 115
    rite of passage, 126
    social media, 40
Anti-Defamation League, 7, 12, 26, 113, 147
    Pyramid of Hate, 12
Antisemitism
    against Israel, 69, 72–73, 78, 82
        3D test, 72–73
    definition, International Holo-caust Remembrance Alliance, 124
    delegitimization of the Holo-caust, 22
    in France, 91
    intersectionality, 102, 106
    Jewish choices, 147
    from the Left, 70–71, 74–78, 85, 145, 148–149, 151
    microaggression, 11–12, 41, 50, 133–134
    online, 44–49
    in peer groups, 8–10
    post-Holocaust antisemitism, 148
    responses to, 60, 135, 138, 149, 151
    from the Right, 21, 70–71, 77–78, 85, 145, 148–149, 151
    in schools, 5–7, 25, 28–29, 33, 42–43, 97, 132

Black Death, xi
Black Lives Matter, 42, 45
B'nai mitzvah, 2, 126, 129
    Black Mitzvah, 103–104
    spiritual moment, 139
Boycott, Divestment, and Sanctions Movement, 81–82

Code Switching, 95
COVID-19, 4, 14, 30, 39–40, 48, 77, 93, 98

Dyke March, 74–75, 77
    Chicago, 2017, 74
    Washington, DC, 2019, 75

Generation Z
activism, 146–147
COVID-19, 48
demographic cohort, 4, 12, 14,
117, 123, 134
gun violence, 60
Holocaust knowledge, 13, 21,
31–32
Israel, 77–78, 84–85
and Now study, 10
parents, 8, 79, 93–95, 112–115,
117, 141
social media, 40–41, 43, 49–50,
147

Holocaust
concentration camp, 19, 21,
26–28, 30, 58
comparison to U.S. detention
facilities, 26–27, 32–33
denial, 13, 31, 47–48
Eva Stories, 45
Frank, Anne, 34, 46–47
Hitler, Adolf, 10, 19, 31–33, 42,
47, 147
Holocaust education, 6, 22–24,
27–33, 60
Mengele, Joseph, 19–20
Never Again, 20–21
as part of Jewish identity, 34,
123
Polenaktion, 55–56
on social media, 39–40, 45–48
Stolperstein, 55
survivors, 19, 22, 28–29, 39
swastika, 28, 42, 103, 113, 118
Holocaust Education Bill, SB 664,
27–29

Identity
in adolescence, 6–7
cooking, 130
Erickson, Erik, 123
formation, 123
Gee, James, Theory of, 9
Jewish identity, 3, 8, 10, 34, 75,
90, 98, 104–105, 116,
122–125, 137–141
minority identity, 135
politics, 150
racial identity, 108–109, 134
Israel, 70–74, 81–82, 146
history, 70
Israeli-Palestinian Conflict,
70–74, 81, 146
Nakhba, 70
War of Independence, 70
Zionism, 72, 74–75, 80, 82
as racism, 49

Judaism, 3, 7, 118, 125–127,
130–133, 136, 141
Amalek, 20, 149
Ashkenazi Jews, 44–45, 102
Heschel, Abraham Joshua, on, 1
interfaith families, 113, 116
Jewish education, 2–3, 10, 51,
115–116, 152
Jewish family, 122, 136–137
Jewish identity, 3, 7–9, 25, 45, 75,
92–94, 96–98, 105, 116, 119,
122–125, 127–128, 131–132,
134–135, 137, 139, 141
Haddish, Tiffany, 104
whiteness, 134
Jewish Pride, 74, 93, 114–115,
139

Jewish ritual, 107, 115, 128–129
Jewish star, 90
Jewish stereotypes, 13, 77, 85,
    104–106, 135
  dual loyalty, 85
  nose jobs, 104–105
Jews of color, 102–104,
    106–109
Judaism and the internet, 50, 71
kosher dietary practices,
    128–131
  Kosher Soul, 130
Lipstadt, Deborah, on, 9
remembering the Holocaust, 21
self-hating Jews, 80
Shabbat, 18, 127, 131
Torah, 20, 98, 139, 150, 152

Millennials, 13, 31, 48–49, 126,
    156
  Holocaust knowledge, 13, 31
  news consumption, 48
  social media, 49
  unbundling, 126, 156

Nazis, 10, 20, 25, 31–32, 55–56
  neo-Nazis, 148

Pew Research Institute, 21, 31, 34,
    116, 123–125, 130, 134, 147,
    155
  Jewish Americans in 2020, 34,
    116, 125, 130, 134, 147,
    155
  A Portrait of Jewish Americans
    (2013), 21, 123–124

What Americans know about the
    Holocaust, 31

Social media, 6, 30, 32, 39–52, 71,
    147
  antisemitism on social media,
    41–45, 47–49, 147
  Holocaust denial, 47–48
  Holocaust memorialization,
    45–47
  influencers, 12, 41, 49–50
  Instagram, 39, 41–46, 50, 70,
    92, 147
  Eva Stories, 45–46
  memes, 98
  TikTok, 40, 44–45, 47, 71, 105

Tikkun Olam, 57, 96–97, 133
  Clinton, Hillary, 96
  expression of Judaism, 96
  Harris, Kamala, 96
  social justice, 96
Tree of Life shooting, 2, 56–59,
    61–65, 92, 106
  Hebrew Immigrant Aid Society,
    58
  Squirrel Hill, 56, 61, 63–64
Trump, Donald J., 26, 32–33, 44,
    76, 84, 124, 148
Tzedakah, 4

Unite the Right rally, 25

Women's March, 76–77, 93

Zioness, 4, 60, 68, 72, 93, 133, 145

About the Author

Samantha A. Vinokor-Meinrath, EdD, is a lifelong Jewish educator and learner, and currently serves as the Senior Director of Knowledge, Ideas, and Learning at the Jewish Education Project in New York. She is an alumna of the University of Pittsburgh (BA), the Jewish Theological Seminary of America (MA), Gratz College (EdD), and the Pardes Institute of Jewish Studies. Vinokor-Meinrath has worked with Jewish adolescents and emergent adults for more than ten years, serving communities in New York; Washington, DC; Israel; and Ohio. She regularly writes and consults on antisemitism, Jewish teen engagement and identity development, and she was named one of Cleveland's "12 Under 36" Jewish leaders.